COUNSELLING

A Dynamic Approach

DILLIP KUMAR DASH

INDIA • SINGAPORE • MALAYSIA

Notion Press

No. 8, 3rd Cross Street,
CIT Colony, Mylapore,
Chennai, Tamil Nadu – 600 004

First Published by Notion Press 2020
Copyright © Dillip Kumar Dash 2020
All Rights Reserved.

ISBN 978-1-63633-528-5

Contents

Dr. Dillip Kumar Dash

Senior consultant psychiatrist

Apollo Hospitals, Bilaspur

Chhattisgarh, India

Mobile: 9827157323

Email: dillip.dash47@gmail.com

Preface

This little book of few lines is not just about everything but is the sum of everything of traditional counselling. It is the heartfelt composition that I feel sometimes. However, it may not hold true for those who have a contradictory view. These few lines of this book are the way I taught myself to grow a little ahead towards my consciousness. I got to know a lot from those who disagree.

We should know life before we lose it. No one can give the details of the divine truth. It has to be accepted as it is. Nothing was serious as I realized I have a little more time in my hand and a new life to cherish. This is when I started living life. In summarizing, I stated a few aspects of human life in this book with an experience of more than two decades in the field of counselling.

These few quotations, explanations evoked by positive thoughts, ways of spiritual guidance as explained in Bhagavad Gita, Kabir's couplets, and contemporary counselling techniques are of psychotherapeutic/traditional counselling approach which I follow in my clinical practice. You can follow these few lines for an eternal approach to counselling your clients.

I also tried to summarize the brighter, lighter, and darker aspects of life in a few quotations considering the values.

I have been working with clients needing psychological help for around 20 years and apart from medicinal therapies, my major way of treatment is giving counselling and structured psychotherapy. However in India, the number of patients per psychiatrist is high in proportion, so a traditional way of counselling is a better option which I realized and the same I am practising rather than opting for structured psychotherapies always.

In contemporary psychiatry, psychotherapy, and counselling this is my own revelation of using the terminology "Traditional Counselling." Here I use different self-made quotations, proverbs, and short insight-oriented words for alleviating my clients' symptoms of Depression, Anxiety, Stress, Failure, and even other major psychological illnesses.

I thank everyone that has helped me in my journey and also those whom I do not know but are still a part of my journey. I thank Almighty for his blessings in abundance. I respect the rich and poor, both have shown different aspects of life to me.

If there are some enemies they must be rejoicing my success as I have never injured them. I tried to help those who came across my way. I never earned less than my living and more than my luxury. I have wealth of words than miserly banks. I live with these words and make my clients learn a new traditional way of counselling and prosperity.

A Short Introduction about the Book

This book tells us about the essentials of behavioural, emotional, and spiritual ways of human living. It is my endeavour to find words for these quotations, each of which made me think, contemplate, and even meditate. These are purely the way I counsel my clients.

Every one of us and this book is a creation of the Almighty, essentially is a personification of His art. I talk of life as a celebration because it is the greatest gift that God could give us. We must enjoy life as it comes. In life, there would always be ups and downs, joys and sorrows and triumphs, and defeats. One has to accept and celebrate every moment of life. This is the message I want to convey. It reveals the philosophy enunciated about the inner path. In this brief book, we get a comprehensive picture of our futile ambitions and endeavours which make us unhappy and these words of counselling can wash all our agonies as I presumed and felt in my practice.

This book comprises original psychotherapeutic and traditional counselling concepts, thoughts, and quotes which the reader has to read not only as a reader but as an observer of one's self.

Positive thoughts to ensure achievement and success and the hierarchical use of those are explained here with some insight-oriented suggestions. Controlling and dealing with aggressive impulses and angry outbursts are explained in a very realistic way.

Here, I have also given importance to the suggestions given in Bhagavad Gita by Lord Krishna to Arjuna as classical ways of insight-oriented counselings and are very much akin to transactional analysis, supportive therapy, and cognitive therapy. Similarly, Sant Kabir's couplets are explained how life-oriented those are and their values to attain salvation.

Contemporary therapies like **crisis intervention, marital/couple therapies, TA, cognitive therapy,** are a few which are explained here keeping relevance to my psychiatric practice.

As this book contains materials of traditional, spiritual, emotional, individual (author's) innovative thought implementations and a few technical therapeutic processes it is not possible and also intended to discuss the technical part in detail. Hence this book is highly recommended for reference for the general population, general practitioners, counsellors, psychotherapists, and even for psychiatrists and psychologists.

For a master's course in counselling, psychotherapy, clinical psychology the students need to learn details of explanation of theoretical issues, scientific research methods, and technical issues as well as practical guidelines. Hence in this book, these are not abundantly explained.

Basic Attributes of a Counsellor

- Judgement and respect for other's views.
- Knowledge of analytic skills.
- Working with comfort.
- The ability to work with all human needs, emotions, behaviour.
- Integrating with own assessment.
- Skills in interpreting body language.
- Good knowledge of the language in which the client communicates.

Working Through Process of Counselling:

- Establishing rapport.
- Identifying problem situations and behaviour.
- Assessment of problems.
- Setting goals of the therapy.
- Planning interventions.
- Create self-help skills in the client.
- Explanations of behaviour which are helpful to the client.

Use of Different Counselling Theories

The basic difference between counselling and psychotherapy:

- Counselling emerged from guidance processes like – marriage, educational, NGOs, family contexts.
- Psychotherapy emerged from Freudian psychoanalysis.
- Counselling is less technical and less structured than psychotherapy.
- Psychotherapy is more time consuming than counselling.
- A therapeutic alliance is easy in counselling than psychotherapy.
- Training is lengthy in psychotherapy than counselling.
- Depth of work is extensive in psychotherapy than counselling.
- Personal therapy is recommended in psychotherapy training not seriously in counselling training.

Foreword

Dr Dillip Kumar Dash who fascinatingly written many articles on both scientific and literary has written few beautiful books on counselling and those are of heartfelt philosophical ideas and quotations. His spontaneous spiritual thoughts are reflected in the quotations depicted. He said in an interview that "The way I feel my emotions I make my life to blend into those and on the way I find happiness waiting."

Dr Dash is known to me for the last two decades. He is a philosopher, Doctor, Poet, Writer, and a perfect human being.

He is extending support in many ways to our association & beneficiaries as well. I feel he is extremely close to all human emotions. Dr Dash is hard-working, kind-hearted, and a fine psychiatrist, psychotherapist, and counsellor.

He has published many medical articles in many journals and visited different countries for several training sessions and conferences. His poetic expressions are clearly presented in his writings.

Let all success come to his life.

John Kor
President SWA
Raipur (CG)

Ethical Issues in Counselling

(The issues discussed in this chapter are almost applicable for psychotherapeutic processes, counselling, and also most behavioural therapies)

History

- Counselling is known since ancient ages, that history reveals. It is one of the major sub-faculties in mental health care. In fact, before the era of Psychopharmacological inventions, it was the only mode of effective and humanistic treatment of the mentally ill.

- Since the advent of Psychopharmacological agents no doubt the acceptability of these agents increased, but still counselling is one of the emerging, exciting branches. Due to the huge population diversity in all the areas of human living, gender, cross-cultural bias, and so many other biases and variations counselling take its steps accordingly. Nevertheless, it is the same for all as far as the techniques are concerned.

- Since the emergence of human rights regulations in different countries in recent times there are a lot of debates in mental health care especially in counselling and Psychotherapy and this is the real time to discuss the ethical issues besides the concepts explained.

- Counselling focuses on treating specific disorders rather than changing deeper, underlying personality structures. Although there are many literary works on the effectiveness, most therapies are still in an empirical approach in determining efficacy and effectiveness.

- Long-term Psychotherapies are still practised, but empirical data support better for the short term, directive interventions as primary or adjunctive treatments for specific psychiatric disorders. In addition to their roles as primary and adjunctive treatments for Psychiatric disorders, Psychological inventions may play a substantial role in educating patients about their disorders, explaining treatment rationales, and encouraging them.

Ethical Issues of Great Importance Are:

1. Suggestibility
2. Hostility
3. Defences

However ethical issues differ in many aspects due to varied cross-cultural diversity, one should refer to the depicted codes at least for a therapeutic process to be continued.

Counselling is Offered to Clients If:

- The problem behaviour can be defined in terms of observable behaviour or elicitable emotional labilities.
- The client and the therapist can agree on the clearly defined goals.
- The client understands and agrees with the treatment plan.
- No hazard expected.

Basic Assumptions:

- The empirical validation of therapy.
- The treatment focuses on the here and now of the client's life. The use of explicit agreed and operationally defined strategies.
- The purpose of a code of ethics is to define general principles and to established standards of professional conduct for counsellors in their work and to inform, protect those members of the public who seek their services.
- All counsellors/therapists are expected to approach their work aiming to alleviate suffering and promote the well-being of their clients. Counsellors/therapists should endeavour to use their abilities and

skills to their clients' best advantages without prejudice and with due recognition of the value and dignity of every human being.

- The specification of treatment goals
  (A) Defined changes in the life of the client.
  (B) The use of collaborative therapeutic strategies between client and therapist should always persist.

Ethical Issues: (Activities for Therapist)

Activity Level 1: Ethical issues

- List all the ethical issues that you can recall.

Activity Level 2: Ethical issues

- For each of them, write further two sentences explaining how a researcher might deal with such issues.

  - Research Study to exemplify the issues.
  - Deception in a field experiment.
  - Informed consent in a laboratory experiment.
  - Confidentiality in a survey.
  - The right to withdraw in any kind of research study.
  - Privacy in an observational study.
  - Protection from harm in a psychological experiment.
  - When you are answering a question on ethical issues, ensure that you discuss a good number of ethical problems as well as a variety of different kinds of research.

  - The primary task of therapy is the restoration of the relationship with oneself, the client, and with others and the work.
  - The work of counsellors is conducted through relationships.

Principle of Ethics in Counselling

- The first principle of ethical relationships in counselling is to maintain a healthy and effective working relationship.

- Where there are difficulties, the principle should be to work towards restoring the interrupted or disturbed relationship between therapist and patient if at all possible in the first place.
- Many problems could be prevented from the beginning if a client openly discusses his or her discomforts with the therapist/counsellor, giving him or her the opportunity to change, explain, and seek supervision or other help as needed.
- Supervisors, mediators, or independent consultants could perhaps effectively be involved at the next stage.
- In many cases discussion, working through, insight into the complex dynamics of the therapy can resolve apparent and irrevocable breakdowns.
- Most codes of ethics assume that their purpose is primarily to protect clients from the wrongdoings of therapists.
- We might also consider the need for therapists for protection and help.
- Therapists may sometimes be particularly vulnerable to displaced feelings of vengeance or retaliation for the same complex reasons that doctors who go to help earthquake or other natural calamity victims, may be attacked.
- These primary functions of ethical codes are more educational and protective of the therapeutic relationship.

Code of Ethics:

- Each member organization of Counselling/Psychotherapy should publish a code of ethics that should be approved by their state authorities. Different organizations may have a slight variation in their code as per the organization's requirements.
- **Qualifications**: Counsellors/Psychotherapists are required to disclose their qualifications when requested.
- **Terms, Conditions, and Methods of Practice**: Counsellors/Psychotherapists are required to disclose on request, their terms and conditions, and appropriate methods of practice at the outset of therapy.

- **Confidentiality**: The above practitioners are required to preserve confidentiality and to disclose if requested, the limits of confidentiality and circumstances under which it might be broken to specific third parties.
- **Professional Relationship**: Counsellors should consider the client's best interest when making appropriate contact with the client's GPs, relevant psychiatric services, or other relevant professionals, with the client's knowledge.
- **Relationship with Clients**: Counsellors are required to maintain appropriate boundaries with their clients and to take care not to exploit their clients' current or past, in any way financially, sexually, or emotionally.
- **Publication**: Counsellors are required to safeguard the welfare and anonymity of clients when any form of publication of clinical material is being considered and to obtain their consent whenever possible.
- **Practitioner Competence**: Counsellors are required to maintain their ability to perform competently and to take the necessary steps to do so.
- **Indemnity Insurance**: Counsellors are required to ensure that their professional work is adequately covered by appropriate indemnity insurance.
- **Detrimental Behaviour**: Counsellors are required to refrain from any behaviour that may be detrimental to the profession, to colleagues, or to trainees. They are required to take appropriate action in accordance with the clause, about the behaviour of a colleague which may be detrimental to the profession to colleagues or trainees.

Advertising

- The member organizations in many states/countries are required to restrict the promotion of their work to a description of the type of Psychotherapy, which they provide.
- Counsellors are required to distinguish carefully between self-descriptions as in a list and advertisement seeking inquiries.

- A clear description of "the clinical problem and its treatment" predict better outcomes of inventions for Psychological ailments, would be most essential in Psychotherapeutic procedure.
- Frank – observed many patients shown significant improvement in the process of Psychotherapy by the reassurance process.
- Clear and credible explanations of the patient's diagnosis and treatment plans give more successful results (Kazding Krouse). This also improves the patient's compliance.

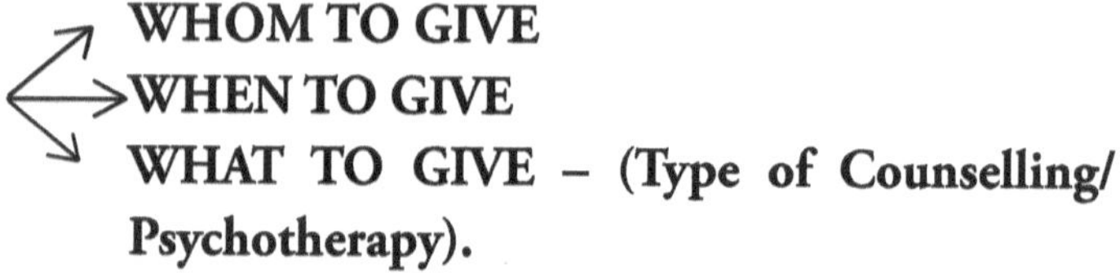

Counselling

- Observation of the patient's behaviour and a Psychodynamic approach should be aimed at the beginning of the session.
- Prior to counselling, an accurate clinical diagnosis is essential. Then the therapist should decide the type of therapy, and what would be better for the client. Different types of therapies can be introduced to patients having the same diagnosis depending on predominant symptoms.
- Clients when behaviourally settled, not showing self-injurious behaviour or hostility can be started with counselling/ Psychotherapeutic approach.

  Example –   Phobia – desensitization

  Major depression – cognitive therapy

  Adjustment discords – supportive & other therapies.

- The therapist should extract the client's hidden symptoms.

WHOM TO GIVE: The clients should have:

1. Adequate suggestibility.
2. No hostility for the therapy and therapist.

3. Appropriate defence mechanisms for therapy.

WHEN TO GIVE: The intensity of the illness should be:

1. Appropriate for a therapeutic alliance.
2. After symptomatic recovery, when the therapist feels it is applicable.

After a proper agreement is done regarding the duration and the approximate number of sessions, fee structure and payment details should be made before the start of counselling/other psychological therapy.

WHAT TO GIVE:

1. After the diagnosis is made the type of therapy should be decided.
2. One or more types of therapies may be considered, but the primary therapy should be considered first.
3. The number, duration, and interval of sessions should be predetermined. However appropriate and necessary changes should be adopted.

e-therapy: Psychotherapy conducted over the internet, e-mail, video phone, or internet phone is also called online counselling, e-therapy, (US online counselling), or online therapy. There are a certain set of laws which govern e-therapy in the US.

Note:

In my clinical practice for more than two decades it has been observed that if the client does not follow, especially the duration between two sessions (Interval), vagueness for sessions earlier than the predetermined duration usually develops a dependency on the counsellor/therapist. The same is for the number of sessions.

If the duration of each session is increased or decreased than the predetermined norms then clients develop transference and counter transferency on the counsellor/therapist. It is mostly seen in some of the demanding clients when the therapist becomes little labile to the norms and the duration is extended than the client mostly develops a positive transferency (like a parent-child-relationship).

Positive transferency helps the client to feel safe to express repressed feelings. Sometimes the counsellor/therapist develops counter transferency on to the client expressing their attitudes and feelings originated outside the therapeutic relationship. This is detrimental to the counselling an analytic procedure.

Counselling Can Help in the Following Ways:

- Clarification of the problem and how to maintain symptomatically.
- Analysis of motivation of the client, giving access to incentives.
- Self-analysis gives strength to the client to participate in therapy.
- Analysis of Socio-cultural and Physical environment.

Other issues which are important in counselling/other psychological therapies:

- Therapists/counsellors from the same cross-cultural, racial, socio-economic backgrounds as the client are favourable than of different backgrounds.
- Proper training is required for Therapists/counsellors and even more required is an inborn quality of being a good therapist.
- Having a sense of developing a good therapeutic alliance.
- A proper diagnosis of psychiatric illness should be made to decide the type of therapy.
- Separate research criteria should be made which may differ from the clinical therapeutic criteria.

Ethical Codes:

- Set ethical behaviour, and principles of guiding behaviour.
- Set guidelines for practice.

- Desire to protect the clients and the profession.
- There are predetermined, created, and voluntary innovations. These are predeterminable and decided by state or other registered organizational bodies.

Ethical Committees

- Major organizations do have their own ethical committees. Most ethical committees do adjudge the ethics violation.
- The ethical committee investigates, obtains evidence, and conducts meetings for hearing with the concerned parties.
- The ethical committee may suspend, reprimand, revoke the counsellor/therapist.
- The state/organizational board can be notified if found a violation of ethical issues by the central ethical committee.

Ethics are rules which should be compiled by the state, organizational board, and board members for universal/common betterment.

Laws Involved

1. Criminal Law: Ensures the associated violator up to the sentence of sending him/her to jail.
2. Civil Law: Does have provision for monetary fine, suspending from a job, and other associated professional sanctions.

Usually, the ethical issues are not associated with strict laws that can take the counsellor to the court of the law barring severe criminal issues involved and/or severe professional negligence which can damage the client's life.

If legal issues to be considered:

- Lawyers are involved.
- The Court of law is the place of judgement.
- The counsellor would be in danger of misconduct.

Most of the time in ACA (American Counselling Association) the ethical issues involving legal contempts are resolved within the state/organizational bodies.

Defining the standard of practice is very important for legal actions.

Working through the code of Ethics stepwise:

1. Rapport with the client.
2. Confidentiality of the client, privacy.
3. Encouraging communication.
4. Professional responsibilities.
5. Liaison.
6. Evaluation and interpretation of the counselling/psychological therapies.
7. Systematic supervising process.
8. Training (promote professional growth).
9. Research.
10. Resolving Ethical issues.
11. Maintaining personal values which are not deterrent to clients.
12. Prohibition of any sort of assault on clients.
13. Protection of client's rights in research and publication.
14. Helping clients to obtain self-determined goals.

(– ACA code of ethics 2005)
(– Kotter and Brown 1992)

Ethical/legal issues: A focus

1. Informal consent
2. Occasionally written consent
3. Confidentiality
4. Reprimand
5. Making an ethical model for use
6. Record keeping
7. Technology

- Confidentiality is the trusting foundation of counselling. It is not a privilege.
- The client's risk assessment is essential. For example: The client is suicidal or homicidal.
- Record keeping in counselling practice

Wheeler and Bertrasam (2008) found the following important purposes:

a. Clinical/therapeutic management.
b. Legal issues for the client.
c. Protection of other health-related information.
d. Emergency/Risk management.

Ethical Decision Making:

a. Early identification and discussion of significant issues.
b. Always it should be according to a state/organizational/national code.
c. Involve your colleagues to discuss the dilemma.
d. Keep choices for a different course of action.
e. Evaluation of the final course of action.
f. Implementation of course of action.

Morality associated with ethics of counselling is a "belief" which makes the counsellor believe what is right and what is wrong.

Ethical Moral Principles:
a. Autonomy: The client's right to be preserved.
b. Nonmaleficence: No harm to the client.
c. Beneficence: Promoting welfare to the client.
d. Justice to the client.
e. Loyalties to the client.

(COUN 540: Foundations Spring 2009)
Additional qualities the counsellor should have:

a. Self-awareness: Of their own health, of what they are providing.

b. Empathetic: To communicate with the client's core feelings.

c. Desire to help.

d. The value system of the counsellor should not be detrimental to the client.

Corey – Cautions both endpoints of

i. Holding absolute belief and exerting influence on clients to adopt the above points.

ii. Attempting to be value-free.

Qualities of a Counsellor

1. During the procedure in general, should have equality feeling with the client, his/her relatives, and the significant others.

2. Should respect and realize the client's behaviour without any confrontation.

3. Should able to establish rapport.

4. Should give acceptable information/opinion regarding the client's concern and should have soothing behaviour towards the client.

5. Should understand the client's routine life without showing expressed emotions.

6. Should respect the client's social values and also may act as a social mediator for the client.

7. The therapist should maintain a democratic relationship with the client which should not be dominating or conflict generating for the clients.

8. Should be trusted and accepted by the client.

9. The client's need for help should be confidential and respected.

Achievement/Success

All achievements are dependent on motivation.

Basic psychological aspects which increase motivation:

- Desire of:
- Life, love, growth.
- Impulses, aggression.
- Marriage, sex, death.
- And hope for a better life after death.

Plan your action for the future and do not neglect today's achievement even if it is too small.

- Think with hope.
- Set a goal.
- Start from small actions to bigger.

You may get few failures and those would be the real markers of your achievement.

Share all your success, achievements, and credits with others.

Understand the qualities of a successful person and follow his ways of success. Regular observation of the activities of a successful person and applying those to self will definitely help realistically.

Achievement is a mishap for an idle man who always says he is busy for the other reason. So do not be idle and hope for success.

Do not say what you can do for others; say what you can do for yourself.

Hope high even if you may fall too much lower in your goals. Life's experience is a continuous process.

Sometimes you may go forward, sometimes a little backward.

Your goals initially should be realistic and getable. For long-term achievements, you should have a continuous process of improvement, which may be very slow.

As an individual, you look for personal growth in your personality, and working abilities. Improve your mental setup and your emotionality.

Modify yourself for getting achievements in your life.

- According to your goal make your mental state and thoughts.
- Plan your time.
- Make your physical being healthy
- Find out easier ways to sort your job and find a way towards the goal.

Steps of Achievement

a.   Planning of goal (preferably one at a time).

b.   Analyze your dreams.

c.   Bring your dreams to action.

d.   Appropriate placement of your thoughts into ideas.

e.   Convert your ideas gradually to the goal.

a.   Make a routine (time table) to finish up your work by strict principles of timeliness.

b.   Have a sense of emergency in your job.

c.   Make a checklist of your work.

Never compare yourself with others. Think you are the boss of your own and you can do the best of your capabilities no matter what others can do.

Use your time constructively before and beyond success. Apart from your job, sleeping hours, rest of the time you use meticulously for your eternal, physical, social growth. Those will give you a feeling of euphoria.

Recall your smaller achievements during bigger and tougher tasks. Stepwise proceed on your work and if possible you may take others' help.

Rehearsal of one act and using your brain in different works can give you more options for a reward.

Make a time table for each day.

In between your work, make your mind a little relaxed.

Steps to developing will

1.   Committing intellect to definite goals.
2.   Repetitive power of Habit.
3.   Concentration.
4.   Positive direction to vital energies.
5.   Detached work.

Trouble proneness is the personality of some people and their mind is always attached to worrisome acts.

Remove worries from your mind as those are more threatening than your enemies. Worries are basically – illogical, for some vague reasons, and difficult to deal. So to reduce your worries you eliminate the source of expecting a loss. Once the worries are eliminated even with a minimal loss do not mind and do constructive works. Those will pay you more.

For success:

Do: – Planning.
         – Accumulate your knowledge in the process.
         – Preparation for the final step to be done.
Do not: – Hope for an overnight success.
         – Dishearten of doing long years of hard work.
         – Expect a reward immediately.

Life is just what we structure it through our acts. All events in life make our destiny (success or failure).

Do something every day and during the journey of your life, you will do a thousand things. Most of your doing would reflect lots of positive things through the journey of your life.

For a positive growth in your success and achievement, you do your current job and think for a future higher job where you want to go. Repeated rehearsal of the higher job avenues in your mind will make you ready for the same in near future.

Do every justifiable thing by searching time. Do not think time to be available for you.

If you are happy during your difficult time, you can be successful.

Time Management

1. Perseverance.
2. Share tasks or problems with others.
3. Avoid Procrastination.
4. Use a time log.
5. Take regular breaks.
6. Create Habits.
7. Priorities.

8. Avoid distractions and interruptions to your work.
9. Action planning.
10. Keep a to-do list.
11. Review your progress.

When a strong defeat comes, take a little break for a few days and think fresh, start your way fresh and you will find success somewhere waiting for you. Even in those days of defeat, do not forget your own identity and stick to your ideas.

The more you go strong along with your failure you will have a positive effect on your future success.

If you desire success and face a failure, follow the below steps:

- Increase or stay on your confidence.
- Repeat your perseverance.
- Find where you defaulted.
- Understand the reason for your failure.
- Gather more and more knowledge regarding your work.
- Think that you are the source of your failure and you have the seeds of success.

For success
    – Gather knowledge, analyze it.
    Make new ideas, do mental practices of those ideas.
    Be sure what you are doing and what you want to do.
    Finally, implement all your knowledge into practice. Repeat practising and your experience will pave a way.

Gather relevant information, data, and values.
Discuss it with your friends.
If you find it positive make a decision on that.
Holistic decision making will give a better result.

Self-understanding including your thoughts, ideas, impulses, and desires will make you feel like a person where you stand.

Believe in them whom you know and have high self-esteem which you can justify. These can increase your success rate.

Find a positive aspect of everything you face and cultivate those in your mind.
Some day you will find the entire thing as positive.

Do not believe in body language as those are inconclusive.
Listen to the words.
Have direct communication that would increase your fact realization.
Either you fail or pass, your brave attitude is above both. If you fail it is your braveness which will give positive thoughts for the future and there may be a huge success. If you pass your attitude would be attracted by many.

Believe in yourself, trust others, and surrender to the Almighty. This will take care of your fear of failure, apprehension for others, and uncertainty of the future.

Especially for students, one to one interaction with teacher and family members is necessary. Have a discussion to make a chart of your job to do. **The self discussion should be a part of every student's performance and it also applies to others**.

Achievements are dependent on your attitude towards life. If you are assigned something, never feel you are too old to do this. Because it is just a mental factor as far as success is concerned.

Your failures are your past. Now at present, you are always new with new ideas, contents, people, and tasks. So hope for a better result.

If you can change your ideas from good to better, foes to friends, illness to well-being, you can change your being from aged to young.

Advises are fruitless until those come from wise and unto the wise.

Look at the pages of history you will find many successful people accepted all odds as encouraging for their success.

Any work which is a task to prove your ability may generate some anxious moments. But these anxious moments if not dealt with properly would lead to worries and frustration and failure. So remove these anxious moments or convert those into assertiveness.

Be persistent on each success. By doing this, your attitude and behaviour will be positive.

When you find it difficult with your neighbours, do not change your house, do not fight with them, and do not avoid them. Just change your attributions from **disliking to liking**.

- Change your way of thinking.
- Change the behavioural patterns.

One of the most valued aspects of the personality of a successful person is that he rationalizes other's arrogance, ill behaviour as not for him, maybe for some other person.

- Never show any anticipatory behaviour especially of anger.
- Learn to reconcile.
- Speak less in a confronting situation, so that you can save your mental energy, which can exhibit a soothing behaviour and you may earn a new friend.
- All the way you can save a lot of time.

You are the actor; you are the dictator and the achiever for your own glory. Just be a little cautious about your own job/work/act.

Start your own work, may face failures or flourish. Just be a little responsible throughout as if you are curing your own illness.

If you have thought many times over your act as right, stick to it even though there may be some noise around you. Be calm. You may find some stoppages throughout your journey. And there is your chance to grow. Start thinking about how to plan for taking a step ahead. Put your efforts and success is there at the next stop.

Have: Positive dialogue with self.

- Devotion to your work.
- Dream your success.
- Demand more from your own actions. Destiny will be on your way.
- Work little wisely and no aimless activities. All those will take you to sovereignty.

Thousand of thoughts will come to your mind every day. Few get filtered at the unconscious and subconscious mind. A few thoughts will be left behind and you decide which one to be attempted with priority.

- Act one by one.
- Better ideas nurtured gives better achievement.

Saint Kabir says "He who can dare to burn in the fire can live near a Master." This is the way a person who despite difficulties tries to persist in one act can have success in the future.

There are many good things behind the curtain. Just go a little inside it. This is the mantra of success.

Closely observe your next-door neighbour who succeeded and the steps he followed.

You will only be helpless when you dishonour others and their achievements. So develop respecting behaviour for others' success and achievements.

Mantras of Success

- Observe others' success. The path they travelled until their achievement.

- Desire your own success.
- Simply admire the person in front of you who had success.
- Try to achieve more or the same which your next-door achiever had.
- Everybody follows someone. So you follow someone. The followers follow the reason, not exactly the person.
- The most important is what you desire should be worthy of your life.

For every success and achievement, it needs to have encouraging reinforcement from others.

As a child, everyone should learn to live in hardship and work hard to find a way to succeed. Too much lavish living can spoil the child.

Consider the good qualities of a person keeping aside his negative qualities and that will make you learn other's good qualities which will give you some success in future

Achievement is not your continuous success. It is your success after each of your failures.

Your achievements are just one less than the maximum. So try for the future.

To become successful you should know yourself.

Your failure often creates tough times for your relatives. So it is advisable not to give much importance to the success and failure rather your efforts for the next event should start now. Think that every failure can have future success. The whole suffering of your failure is nothing but an emotional attachment to the failure and the desire for success. In a problem situation, you have to reduce the emotional attachment as well the desire.

For everything in your life you have to take initiative and not hope that a crown is ready for you of not being announced as a king.

- Keep yourself away from talking too much about your plan.
- Listen to others with patience and grab a few good points.

We hardly get success trying to conquer stress. If we try to know how to cope and change the ways of our thinking, nothing will act as a stressor.

Know what you can do, and then you can measure the ocean and sky.

Take one step in going, complete it at once. Do not handle too many at a time.

- Make smaller parts of big tasks and perform separately. Your appreciation of the act is important and your attitude makes a result out of it.

To become happy the first thing is to have a positive attitude. Be graceful and tidy. Talk to your friends and associates cheerfully. Be confident about your work and you will generate more positivity. Even when you feel low try to behave cheerfully and after some time you will actually become cheerful. Most of the time what you repeatedly do your mind accepts those and after some time your real being becomes somewhat like that.

Reinforce your positive thoughts, ideas, and behaviour even though those may be too little. The sum of all your behaviour will make a big difference and your entire personality will become positive. And positive personality always gives positive growth.

Mind it you are the first person who can help yourself. The world would be of secondary help. You may find a failure or a success once you attempt a challenge. **And both in failure and success there remain a deep inspiration**.

To get success, you have to first attempt your given task.

Every morning look at the mirror and see your smiling face.

- Start the day believing that today you can do at least better than the worst.
- Talk to yourself. Things will go positively even if in the lowest intensity.

People need others because of their own insecure feelings regarding their existence and constantly need an appraisal from others. Rather they should act at their own job independently and regard their own self. Regard yourself and then you will spread a generous attitude to others. At last people around you will regard you as well they will get bothered for you.

Do not think that you can give the world to others. You can give others what you have and without knowing those, the qualities would be wasted. So know yourself.

Your love and passion for others is your success. It allows you to be cared for by more people and you get help in your necessity. Hence you are the creator of your own peace, success, and achievement.

When you suffer from depressive disorder many negative thoughts come to your mind. You may feel helpless, hopeless, and worthless. Now is the time you try to find your positive qualities. Find your likings and assert them on those. During the course of time, you may find happiness. Those little feelings of happiness would create your success story.

Most often in depressed people their self believe is low. They cannot accept that they can complete their job. Our mind at any of the stages – unconscious, subconscious, or conscious – will always try to find a way for success. We have to believe that we can do the job. The reward will come a little late. This is convincing counselling for those who suffer from depression.

For any success there has to be:

- A job to do.
- Thoughts and ideas of performance.
- Plan of action.
- The belief of being capable.
- Act properly till it is complete.

The majority of psychological (neurotic) illnesses can be handled properly with a positive thought if you talk to yourself with positivity and intent for getting through. During a repeated rehearsal the coding of memory becomes intact and your mind accepts it.

Once your mind accepts something it would be definitely a reality.

Knowledge depends on the calmness of the mind.

There are 4 faculties of the mind:

1. Manas
2. Budhi
3. Chitta
4. Ahankar.

Manas – Sankalp, Bikalpa, Anta karan

Causative mind.

Thinking mind.

The mind is the primary instrument of perception, interpretation.

The mind is Prakriti – the absolute nature. So it is ever-changing.

The mind is in constant flux, that's why it is difficult to control.

The mind is a set of variables.

Techniques of Mind Management:

1. Objectifying the thoughts – metacognition. Do not identify with the thoughts.
2. Enhance your awareness.
3. Yogic process – use of vital energies to higher levels.
4. Regulating life – Daily routine should be systematic.
5. Share your joy with others.

- Dharma
- Artha   } Basics of human personality
- Kama
- Moukshya

6. How to handle negativity.

7.   Managing stress – Meditation.

8.   Decision Making

5 Practical Tips to Mind Management:

- You rewire your Brain through your mind (thoughts).
- Think positive
- Eat healthily
- Keep your mind active and learn new things.
- Exercise

Motivation

Maslow's Theory of Motivation:

- This theory explains – A hierarchy of motivation leads to self-actualization.
- Motivation is inertia that intends to satisfy different human needs.
- The kind of work should be based on classic economic theory and human motivations can be revolutionized by accepting the reality of higher human needs including the impulse to self-actualization and the love for highest values (Huffman – 1989 p. 255).
- According to Maslow, a satisfied need can no longer motivate. Example – When hungry people are fed they are no longer motivated by the prospect of food, but when hunger returns they are re-motivated.
- Maslow's research on motivators did not found effective in black foot Indians are Canadian tribes who are very much lack of motivation. Their possessions, wealth is meaningless to them. So they willfully donate it to who so ever requires it. 80-90% of the black foot tribal people are ego secured people.
- Talent as a drive for motivation
- Talent is the possibility of developing a skill. It is also a drive, a need and thus it is potential. This will lead to achievement, success, and reward.
- Theory of hierarchy of human needs Behaviour, motivation, and achievements are dependent on human needs. All needs when remaining in a hierarchical stage gives the best result.

1. Basic psychological needs – Hunger, thirst, sex.
2. Security needs – Once the needs of hunger, thirst, and sex are fulfilled the awareness are deepened for security needs. This is for overall safe living.
3. Belongingness needs – This is to avoid social anxiety, loneliness. If these are not fulfilled there are risks of failure and maladjustment.
4. Self-esteem – High self-esteem is generated by our achievement and the more is the achievement the more self-esteem. Lower self-esteem is the need to know.
5. Cognitive needs – Distorted thoughts are modified by cognitive therapy.
6. Self-actualization.
7. Aesthetic needs.

- If the only tool you have is a hammer, it is tempting to treat everything as if it were a nail.

  North American Proverb – Maslow Psychology
- Hang a thief when he is young, and he'll not steal when he's old

  – 1832 A. Henderson (Scottish Proverb).

  – Used as a motivational theory.

Maslow's Hierarchy of Needs

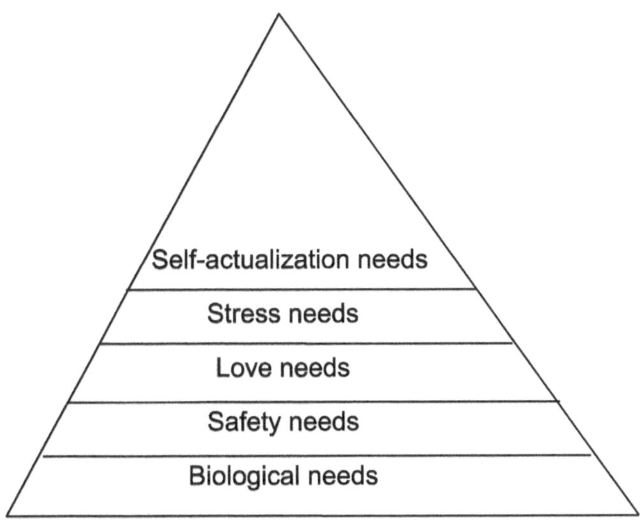

How Action Develops character

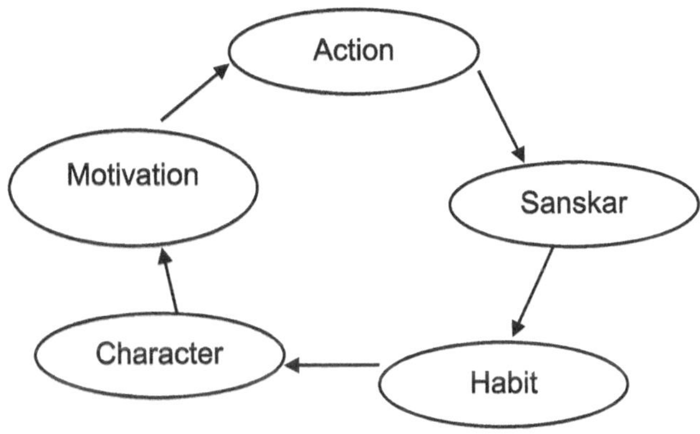

Depression: A Dynamic Approach

To hate is the most negative thing in life. Because you do not like a man is no reason he is your energy; this is a busy world, and none of us has time to sit down and hate one another. The idea that a man has enemies is, after all, only egotism gone to seed. – Hubbard

You are honest by your innate nature and stand up to it. Some day honesty will shower as well-being.

Your mind is working always. Your behaviour is visible everywhere. Every time you create another space towards love and eternity. Spread rose petals to others at least in your thought. And the kindness of God would be evident in the next step.

You, yourself are your finest friend and biggest enemy. So stay conscious about your own thoughts and act with judgement in a hope of getting some positive news in the future.

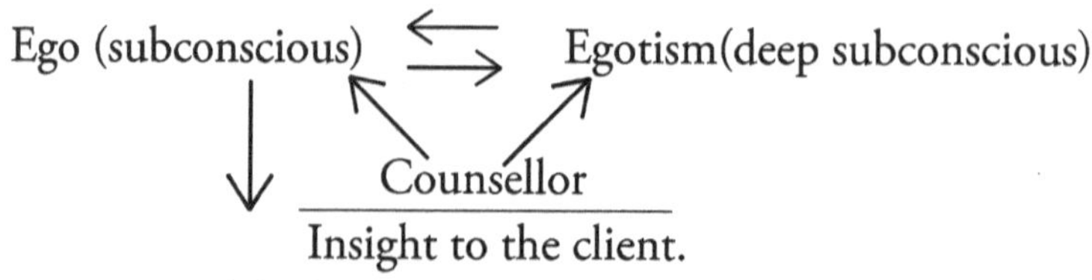

Model of ego counselling.

Whenever you feel you are left alone, be silent; do not use your thought processes too much. Give as much time as you can give to yourself to remain silent and in the course of time, there would be self-realization. And beyond it, happiness would be waiting. You become spiritual now. The next stage which comes automatically is the stage of meditation. Meditation requires:

1. Remaining in silence.
2. Observe your own thoughts and emotions.
3. Searching self-help from within.
4. Remain alone for some time every day.
5. Remain close to nature.
6. Lastly, just observe and observe your internal functions like breathing and the heartbeat with a conscious mind and a time will come where you will be free from all thoughts.

All these together contribute to meditation. There are different types of meditation. Different types of meditation are beneficial for different types of behaviour like – Insomnia, depressive symptoms, anger, and irritable behaviour.

Any symptom/behaviour which makes you feel sad, lethargic, hopeless, guilty, irritability, and sometimes aggressive:

- Just feel those.
- Think to find a way out of those.
- Act on those gracefully every day till those passes away from you.

✱ ✱ ✱

The agonizing mental pain of any kind can be diminished when you start doing some job which requires both physical and mental labour. Because now the brain can tell you even in times of so much mental pain I can work differently which allows you to work something else and gradually the distressing feelings are washed out.

Every behaviour is a result of some thoughts. Negative thoughts multiply at a higher rate than positive thoughts. Negative thoughts dominate the mind more often than positive thoughts. Every mind at some point in time does have positive thoughts and if you think over, those will create more space for positive thoughts and your behaviour will be more goal-oriented.

People who have sadness for some reason, anxiety, despairing cry, obsessive thoughts and insomnia, should give a little space for a positive thought for some time and think over keeping behind hundreds of negative thoughts. For sure your positivity will increase.

During the period of stress, talk to your own self. Go out to open space. Look at the beauty of the sky and the earth. Tell yourself that the universe is unending and your little problem can only occupy a little space and rest is for all positivity in life.

Every time you do a job, find a little rest period and accumulate energy. It can be used in another finer act.

Believing in self is the first step for success. Doubting self is the first step for failure. In both positive faith and doubt, the mind is prepared accordingly and you get the result.

If you are facing troublesome anxiety, worries, fear, depression, and related symptoms, the first thing that you nourish in your mind with assuring positive thoughts. Feed your body with food when it is sick and hungry. Think that with every step you take, you learn something positive.

Your depressed physical look, poor confidence gives an indication to others regarding your current status and poor ability. So many times, in many instances, many people will reject you. So be confident and cheerful even though you know that you are depressed. Repeating this will give you inner positive thinking. Always find your positive points even though you may have negative aspects. Work on your positive aspects and you will find a way to resolve your negatives.

If you can retrieve from your memory your successful days during your stressful time and only if you can act on these, definitely you will get a positive result.

Failures give maximum opportunity to learn. A student or for that matter anyone who wisely accepts failures and willfully tries to learn from those, the defeats last for short period.

If you have faced a failure think that one obstacle is gone and find the ways out of that which can lead you to many successes.

Just do not belittle the work of a student by finding a small mistake. The first thing to find his positive works and at the end, you can just hint him his negatives only if you can suggest him to rectify those.

Positive reinforcement is also rewarding for the person who is giving it because:

- It projects a healthier attitude.
- He is acknowledged with respect.
- It gives mental tranquillity and hence his future acts also become positive.

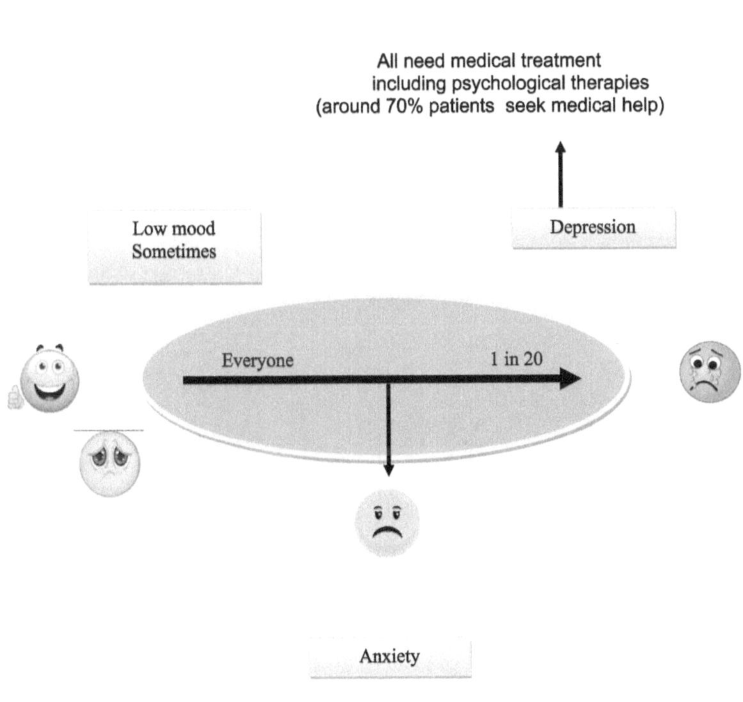

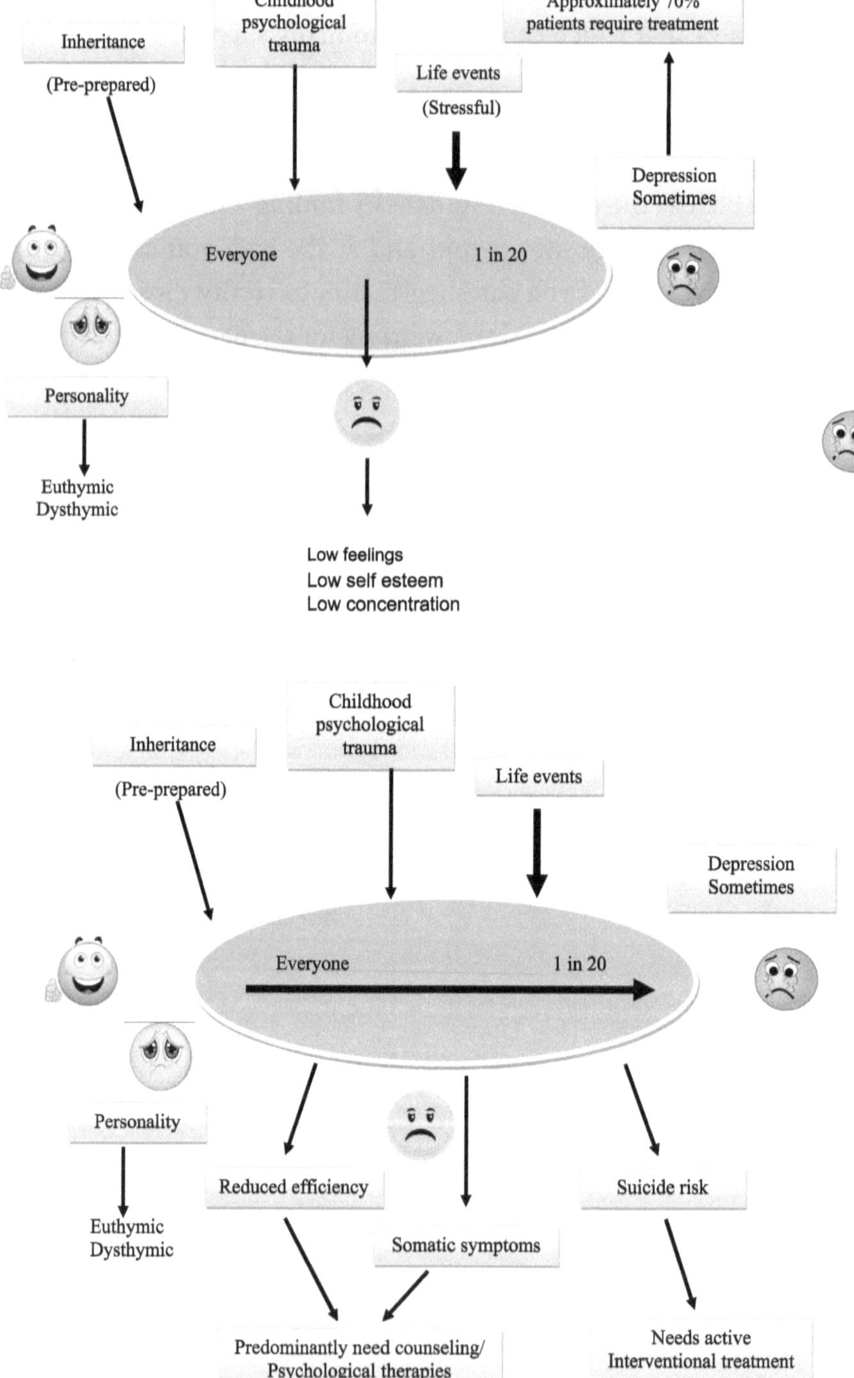
Inheritance
(Pre-prepared)
Childhood
psychological
trauma
Life events
(Stressful)
Approximately 70%
patients require treatment
Depression
Sometimes
Everyone
1 in 20
Personality
Euthymic
Dysthymic
Low feelings
Low self esteem
Low concentration
Inheritance
(Pre-prepared)
Childhood
psychological
trauma
Life events
Depression
Sometimes
Everyone
1 in 20
Personality
Euthymic
Dysthymic
Reduced efficiency
Somatic symptoms
Suicide risk
Predominantly need counseling/
Psychological therapies
Needs active
Interventional treatment

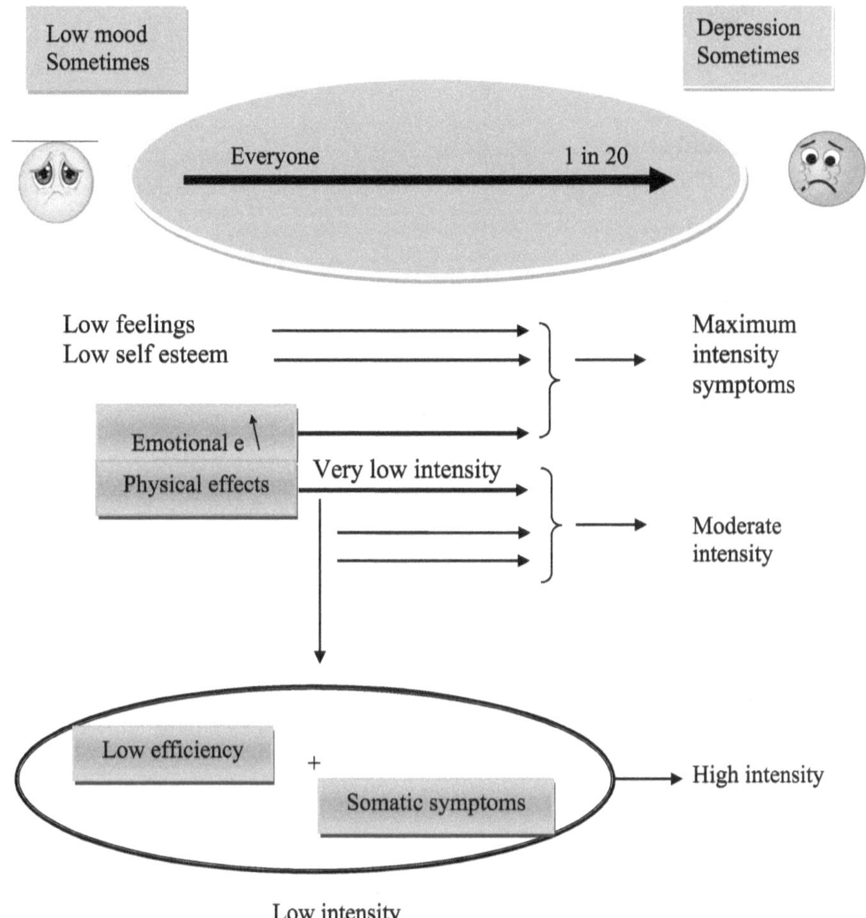

Depression

- An emotion.
- Lability of emotions, if beyond the control of the client it should be diagnosed and treated.
- It is certainly a personal illness.
- It usually starts as a feeling (cardiac neurosis), then it affects the mind and then body.

Predisposing factors are:

- Genetic and family inheritance.
- Type of personality.

- Parenting and upbringing.
- Addiction, job, and other stress.
- Lifestyle.
- Sexual abuse.
- Poor self-image.
- Loneliness.
- Loss.
- Death.
- Failure.
- Interpersonal conflicts.

Depressive Cycle

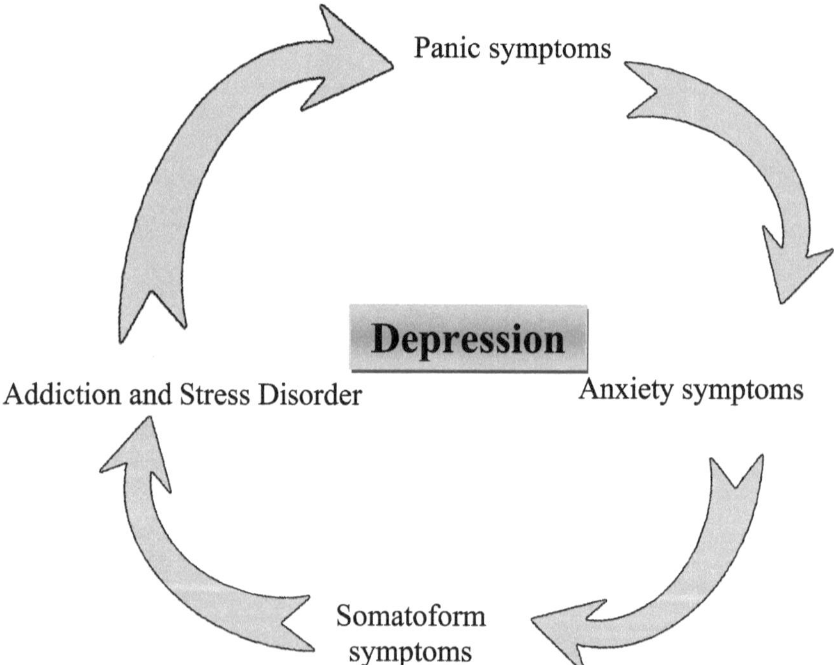

Dealing with depression with psychological therapies:

- Make a trusting relationship.
- Act like a friend.

- Careful listening.
- Supportive counselling and increase motivation.
- Interacting therapies.
- Behaviour therapy.
- Spiritual therapy.
- Medication.
- Referral.

To make a trusting relationship should have

- Core counselling abilities.
- Acceptance by the client.
- Confidentiality.

Listening Carefully

This is the core of any type of psychological therapies, while listening behaves and acts like a friend, give attention to the client's concerns, make a good rapport. The counsellor should work with patience till the end of the therapy session.

Supportive Counselling

The counsellor should explain to the client that the more he/she tells the concern (problem) the more he/she will understand regarding the same. The more the client will understand his/her problem they would be having more coping abilities.

With Supportive counselling, the client understands more about the health issues, and hence the client's coping mechanism, suggestibility towards the counsellor's suggestion, and seeking better opportunities for health issues increase.

In the phase of supportive counselling the counsellor should:

- Behave like a friend with the client.
- Motivate the client's success and commiserate the client's failure.

- Be positive for the future.

Interacting Therapy: Mainly includes –
   a. Preliminary negotiation with NGOs, with private counsellors.
   b. Self-help groups.
   c. Brief therapies.
   d. Other forms of counselling/psychotherapy.

Behaviour Therapy

Cognitive Behaviour Therapy (CBT) is the core therapy which is discussed elsewhere in the book.

Spiritual Therapy

- The clients are always trained to keep their minds at peace. The clients should understand misunderstanding words and wisdom.
- Secondly, the counselling should go beyond the mind to the soul for its well-being. And the soul is the "person in whole."

In the overall counselling of Depression, we should always discuss all three dimensions so that we can treat the client as a WHOLE.

1. Physical dimension – The treatment planned by a medical doctor holistically.
2. Psychological dimension – Counselling, psychotherapy, Behaviour therapy including others should target the client's behaviour, emotion to bring it to a normal state.
3. Spiritual and Religious Dimensions are difficult to handle because of several disparities, disbeliefs in it. But holistically it should be targeted to the core of our soul.

Spiritual and Religious Dimensions should be targeted to have a modification in:

- Self-esteem. This should view to understand the self and also to grow and gain knowledge and wisdom.

- Family and social relations should be dealt with in a give and take way. The person should look to the world and understand his responsibilities towards others. Also one of the major areas of concern should be the attitude towards others and the quality of life.
- Moral values, judgement, and futuristic ideas about life.
- Belief and meaning regarding Life, Death, and God. The counsellor should understand the beliefs and faith of the client and what is his orientation regarding Life, Death, and God. Also if there is a need to change the practice of the client it should be done at an appropriate time with an adequate reorientation process.

It is important to know that the counsellor is not just treating rather he is helping the client to know his/her problems and to seek the way by which he/she can improve holistic health.

Summarizing the Core Issues in Counselling

- Maintaining counsellor and counselee relationship.
- Skilful listening to the client's history.
- Not stating contradicting or biased statements, to the client.
- Giving support and clarifying the client's beliefs.
- Giving positive reinforcement by a few positive words.
- Discuss religious issues freely, which should not impart a negative view of the client.
- With consent from the client, there may be a peer supervisory unit.
- Finding out the area of self-improvement, achievement, and doing a goal-directed therapy.
- To note down session by session improvement and at the end counselling after the required number of sessions give "Thanks to ALMIGHTY."

A subdued patient may show → fragility
                                        ↓
                            Discharged to
Cognitive and perceptual function ← Anxiety ± Depression
↓
Low self-observing capacity   → regressive defences
and conscious orientation   ↓
[H. Davanloo (2002-2004)].   Crying, convention,
                                self-injury, somatization

While giving therapy/counselling to anxious, fragile depressed, and somatized patients it is necessary to build the patient's self-observing capacity so that a proper intrapsychic focus is maintained.

Repeated and continuous projection creates phobia and somatization.

Anger towards mother unresolved
        ↓
Repeated projection   → outward → depression
                             ↓
                             Inward → somatization
Perpetuating anxiety ←

Splitting (defence) views all good or bad to avoid difficult situations people use this defence (splitting).

Depression – Major, chronic with functional ailments like – migraine, GI disturbance, somatoform symptoms: → use regressive defences → Anxiety discharged into smooth muscle → symptoms of cognitive and perceptual disturbance → Low self-observing capacity.

↓ Therapy

(positive) supportive. Build patience and self-observing capacity in the patient. Resolve regressive defences and discard projective defences.

↓ Graded regulation of anxiety

→Bring feelings to the patient's awareness.
  →Let the anxiety symptoms go into
  striated muscles → into smooth muscles

Depressed patients → Unconscious anxiety

   Make the patient aware of feelings

  → Anxiety → striated muscles
   ↓ Repressive defences
   (function: to keep feeling apart)
   ↓ Example: Avoidance, Denial, Displacement,
   Identification, intellectualization, rationalization.
   Isolation of effect.
Depressive symptoms ← Reaction of suppression
    ↓
  Help the patient to feel the anxiety symptoms, see
the Depressive symptoms, and let go of the defences.

Feelings (Exam, Anger) → trigger defences
    ↓
  Depression ← if repressive defences

Depressive patients → Realize the feelings
    ↓ ↑ → evaluate the feelings
 Use repressive ← Anxiety in striated muscles
 and tactical
 defences
   → Anxiety goes to smooth muscles

   ↓ Cognitive perceptual changes ↑
Anger (external) → ↓ Regressive defences

In reactive depression most patients use defences,

exam: Self –Attack (anger turned onto self)

Conversion (suddenly becoming lethargic)

The therapist should point out the causality to the patient and encourage him to fight against the defences and face the feelings. Gradually the threshold to tackle anxiety will increase and simultaneously the realization of feelings will come to perfection and the depressive symptoms will resolve.

How to Deal with the Dynamics of Depressive Patients:

1. Graded feelings:
    - Depressive patients → get into the feelings. Then stop discussing feelings. Then see the reaction.
2. Get back the stimulus from the feelings.
3. Know about the stimulus from the patient and then go into the discussion of feelings.
4. In between the stimulus and feelings there remains the defence. So find it.
5. Make the patient though to defy the defence.
6. In depressive patients, if they use some typical/tactical words that indicate they are using subconscious defences. Sometimes the therapist should support these defences and gradually probe into the feelings.
7. The therapist when asks to talk in detail regarding the stimulus the patient easily analyses the feelings and can control his depressive symptoms.
8. In depressive patients, the defences should be invited before a relapse starts.

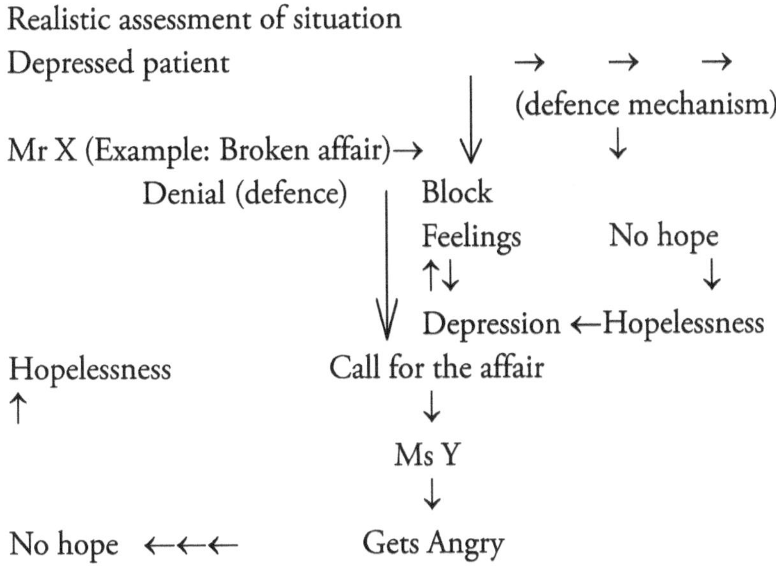

Hopelessness in Depression

Hopelessness is usually created by defences in depressive patients.

Example: A subdued wife gets fired by her husband for being responsible for the poor performance of her child in school. Rather than realizing that she is getting angry she accepts her husband's acquisition (reaction formation) and in the future making herself feel more responsible for the same (self-punishment). She feels she can take all pain for her family ignoring her own anger (Denial).

Repeated use of these defences like – reaction formation, self-punishment, – denial create hopelessness.

- Hopelessness can be a rational response to a loss.
- Hopelessness is irrational because of defences.

Ref: Book –
Co-creating change
Jon Frederickson

Somatisation Syndrome: A Dynamic Approach

The patient's primary complaints are of physical symptoms without identifiable medical aetiology.

Difficulties in diagnosis of somatization syndrome:

1. The Therapist assuming the symptoms as malingering.
2. The therapist not being able to correlate the bodily symptoms and ANS symptoms.
3. The therapist not being able to differentiate bodily symptoms, anxiety, and feelings.
4. The therapist not being able to make a correlation between anxiety and defences.

Some statistical data regarding patients who suffer from somatization:

1. The health care expenses of an individual are 9 times more than an average American's income. (Smith, Monson-Ray – 1986).
2. Somatization patients are sick 2 to 7 days per month (Kartan etal 1991).
3. Only 31 per cent recovered after 15 years of treatment.
4. Suffer the side effects of drugs more than other psychiatry patients.

Brief Historical Background

- Psychosomatic symptoms symbolize an emotional conflict.
- Relates to ancient Egyptians.
- The terminology of SOMATISATION by Stekel 1924

Definition: "The conversion of psychological states into physical symptoms."

S. Freud and Breker – 1974 explained somatic symptoms resulted from traumatic experiences hidden from consciousness.

Somatic symptoms are because of anxiety discharged from autonomic nervous symptoms like:

1. Through striated muscle:

- Acute: Headache, tremors, clenching of hand and teeth, hyperventilation.
- Chronic: migraine, Abdominal and body pain, painful menstruation and intercourse, Globus Hystericus, pseudoseizures.

    ↓

    Psychopathology:

- Feelings from an unconscious impulse
    ↓

    Unconsciously resisting the impulse

2. Through sympathetic nervous system activation:

- Urinary retention, constipation, dry eyes, dizziness,
    ↑ HR, hyperventilation

3. Through parasympathetic nervous system activation:

- Loss or decreased striated muscle symptoms → "jelly legs".
- ↑ urination, defecation
- Hearing and visual impairment
    ↓

    Cognitive/perceptual disruption
    ↓

    Memory dysfunction, impaired consciousness
    (Due to hypoperfusion in the brain)

Chronic use of defences (repressive) gives rise to compromised immune function, increase blood pressure. For patients who use repressive defences, their anxiety is primarily discharged through the sympathetic nervous system. For patients who use regressive defences, their anxiety is primarily discharged through the parasympathetic nervous system.

How to Manage the Somatization Symptoms:

Let the patient realize his defence
↓
Let go of the defences
↓
Face the feelings
↓

1. Anxiety discharged through the autonomic nervous system
    – Breakdown of anxiety will cease striated muscle symptoms
                ↓
    Deal with defence← undermined anxiety goes to
                                        smooth muscle
    ↓   ↓
    Feelings   Deal with feelings
    ↓
    Deal with feelings

2. Somatisation is symbolically identified with the body of the person towards whom the patient has a rage.

How defence work in Feeling, Anxiety, Somatisation, and Depression:

- In individual chapters like Anxiety, Somatisation, and Depression already it is mentioned the use of defences.
- Defences   →   block the reality
                                                                    ↓
                                                    Reality is submerged
Poor adaptability ← recurrent ←   and unsolved
with the situation feelings of unconscious fear
↓

Failure → Depression/Anxiety

Defence Mechanism: A Dynamic Approach

Defences act negatively to see reality, which results in pathological behaviour. (Haan1977).

Example: 1) Patient neglects a treatable illness and later on drops into a serious condition (Denile).

2) Wife being bitten by husband, tells it was immature, he should not have done this – (Intellectualization).

By this, she pushes the anger outside the conscious mind which she cannot accept.

Intrapsychic Development of Defences:

A child since infancy because of the early social learning process learns indirectly that his anxious/irritable feelings make his caretakers anxious. So the child unconsciously uses defences to reduce his feelings.

Most human behaviours are unconsciously driven with automatically guided pre-prepared or procedural memory. (Bargh and Chartrend 1999).

Almost all defences occur unconsciously and hence the therapist has to make the patient aware that he is using the defences.

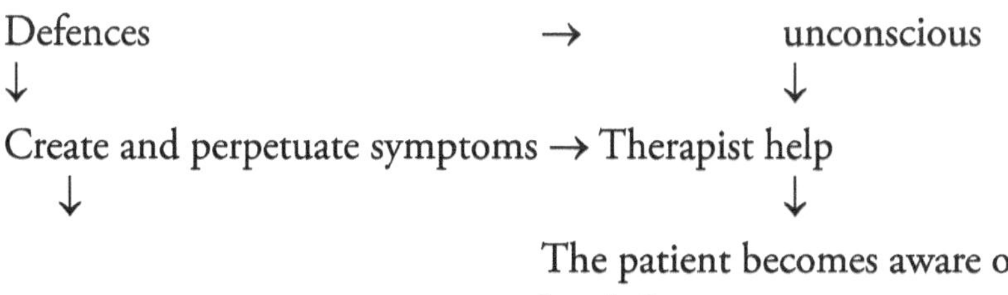

Feelings can be drawn with
$\rightarrow$ The patient decides whether to
use the help of the therapist
those defences or not
$\downarrow$
Most feelings when realized
Do not make use of defences

A patient when uses defences to resolve the internal emotions generated by an external stimulus cannot form a therapeutic alliance.

Patients who are difficult to deal with in a therapeutic process mostly use denial as a defence.

Example; Therapist: What is your problem?

Patient: I do not have any problem.

Every defence mechanism is an act to adapt (Hartman 1964). However most defence mechanisms intrapsychically are attempts to adapt to a stressful situation in an ego satisfying way, but mostly these attempts are maladaptive.

Every defence mechanism does have an ego satisfying positive effect intrinsically.

Example: A person blames himself for not able to save his father from an accident (ego satisfying). But fears his family members would blame him for the cause of his father's death (Maladaptive behaviour).

How to Deal with Defence Mechanisms

Defence mechanisms are:

1. Intrapsychic Phenomena
2. Resolve the conflicts
3. Reduce anxiety

Defence mechanisms work through stages like:

1. Identifying the defences.
2. Clarifying how it is used.

3. Confronting with the defences. Say yourself you are not like your defences.

Defence Therapeutic Work

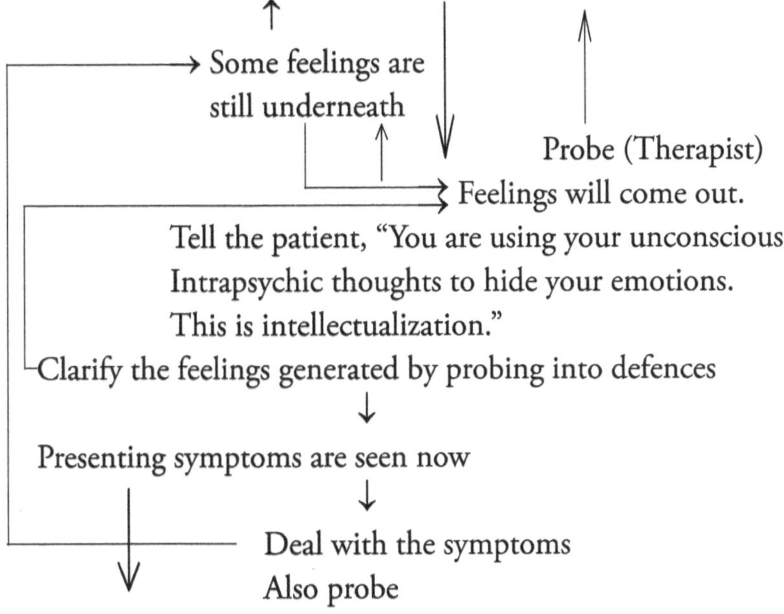

If the patient still identifies himself with his defence
↓
Do not probe the Intrapsychic Phenomenon.

And

Tell the patient, "It is not you, it is how you are not handling your feelings and those feelings are an obstruction to your own self to come out. This is confronting."
↓

Let go of the defences and make the patient realize his own self, the power and the reality of the problems.

Defence Therapeutic Work

Every time you confront a defence if you let go of it you are exploring your own power. So know your defence, confront it and you will find your supreme authorities.

In a therapeutic work if the defence persists → create distancing of patients anxiety and defence

↓

Rapport not properly established ← No signalling of anxiety to make the feelings come up to the surface.

Defence Therapeutic Work

Rapport not properly established

↓

Defence transference is resisted by the patient

↓

The therapist may get annoyed

↓

Rapport is almost not established

↓

Confront the defence transference resistance

↓

The patient realizes he is resisting the defence transference

↓

Patient expresses the defence transference → Therapist makes aware the patient and his defence resistance

Defence resistance resolved ←

↓

Defence

Defence Therapeutic Work

Defence → Defence resolutions with

Therapist tells	– Identification
the patient to	– Clarification
do →	– Confrontation

During defence work, Therapeutic relationship should be tried continuously to improve.

Defensive Mechanism Those Play in Dynamic Theories

Id is unconscious and demands for the instinctual unconscious, the moral drives. Those should be blocked by ego and superego. So there starts conflict, anxiety because of the un-fulfilment of Id demands. However, the person always tries to protect his ego and superego from anxiety and guilt with the use of defences.

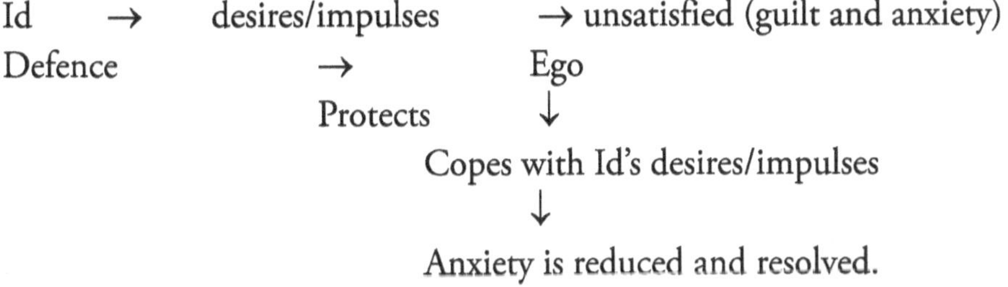

* So defence mechanisms are useful ways for managing stressful conditions and rescuing the conflict and anxiety.

The motive of defence management is to make the patient realize that defences only block their feelings and hide those which later on make more pronounce psychological disabilities.

Types of Defences

1. Mature
   a. Tactical → more interpersonal in nature

b. Repressive → more intrapsychic in nature

2. Immature
   a. Impulsive
   b. Ignorant

Tactical Defences

i. Use of generated words (Feeling upset, nowhere, alone shocked)
   Finally, the feeling comes – Feeling sad

ii. Use of analogous words
   (Oh yes, of course)
   Finally, the feeling comes
   Yes, I felt it.

iii. Diversification: (Use of non-desired words)
   Associating the current matter to a non-desired matter.
   Initial problem: Conflict with husband but during therapy initially the patient will associate with some other member for a different issue.
   Finally, the feeling comes – Yes there is a conflict with her husband.

iv. Use of confusing words (Evasive):
   Giving multiple ways of description.
   (The job environment is: distressing, conflicting, un-mitigating)
   Finally, the feeling comes the job needs too much of technical skill.

v. Use of vague words of symptoms: (Generalization)
   I have a variety of problems
   Not a very specific problem
   Probably a psychological problem, like – Depression
   (Cause of Depression – Loss of job).
   Finally, the feeling comes – I am very much sad.

vi. Use of contradicting words (Undoing):
   Reacting to a situation in two ways contradicting to each other.

(* I am angry.
* Why so?
* No I am not really angry.
* You are contradicting.
* Actually I was angry.
* Now?
* Now Also – Feeling anxious).
Finally, the feeling comes – I feel restless and sad.

Repressive Defences

Intrapsychic in nature

Types:
- Avoidance
- Denial
- Displacement
- Identification
- Repression
- Reaction formation
- Rationalization
- Suppression

Avoidance:
- The patient avoids feelings.
- The therapist in dealing with defences should make the patient face the feelings he avoids and reminds him he just has to feel the feelings and for lifelong the defences would let go.

Denial:
- Denial because of the inability to judge the reality – psychotic/ organic brain syndrome.
- Denial because of to avoid an emotional conflict – Neurotic.

Types of Denial:

a.   Conscious shifting of awareness from an external stimulus which creates fear, anxiety, and or an internal emotion that would create mood changes. Now the patient is not perceiving the external stimulus, anxiety as the patient is not focusing on the stimulus both external and internal.

b.   Negative statements:
Example: The patient failed in an examination. Telling him that he has found out the date of joining in the next class.

c.   Ignoring: Here the actual perspective of the stimulus is not felt in consciousness.

d.   Minimization, (e) Maximization, (f) Generalization.

How to work with denial?

Different types of denial have to be dealt with the situation. However, the core of the process should be to remind his denial of thoughts, ideas, and acts.

Displacement

This is a defence mechanism that works by shifting an emotion to something else. The motive remains unchanged and often it is aggression.

Projection

It is the way of coping with one's undesired motives by shifting them to others.

Example: Thinking to do a wrong thing which makes him guilty and thinks others are doing the same wrong thing –Paranoia.

Identification

Accepting other's views as right.

Repression

- Repressions immediately undo the awareness of a stimulus that causes anxiety.
- Accordingly to Freud, this is the fundamental mental process that reduces anxiety caused by conflicts.

- By this defence mechanism, the person pushes down the feelings of anxiety into the unconscious.
- This uses a lot of psychic energy.
- In later life, the repressed symptoms may take forms like aggression, somatization, or obsession.
- Mostly this defence is used by depressive and psychosomatic patients.
- In repression, there occurs selective memory loss.
- In repression as the primary defence use other secondary defences like Denial, Ignoring Negation, Selective memory loss, lastly Immobility.

Example: Fight with boyfriend.

Using defence:

Step-I – Denial – nothing happened.

Step-II – Ignoring – There was a fight, but that does not bother me.

Step-III – Negation – I have forgotten the event.

Step-IV – Selective memory loss – I cannot recollect what has happened.

Step-V – The fight is still there in the unconscious and the feelings also, but as she is amnesic, she becomes very lethargic and the mobility becomes grossly reduced.

Human beings do have emotional feelings always but the perseverance of defences makes them distract from the feelings by reducing awareness.

Blocked by Defences

Stimulus, feelings ⟶

Experiencing the reality is poor or absent, as the feelings are shifted to unconscious

Remind the patient that he/she is using defences, which he/she should not see the feelings, anxiety. Once anxiety is seen the defences can be tactfully resolved.

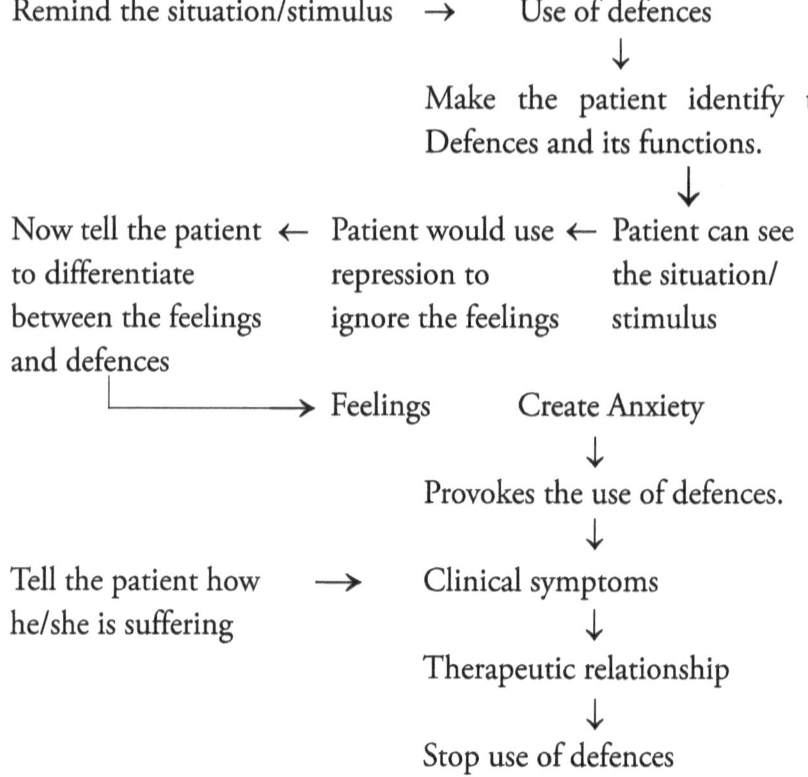

Rationalization

- Substituting the desired motive for an unacceptable work.
- Not lying but putting one's own reasoning.
- Not at the original work/motive, rather a conscious unreal motive.
- A way of creating self-esteem in difficult times.

Reaction formation

Reversal of motives which arouse severe anxiety to cope with conflict; doing the opposite of what he feels.

(Someone taught sex is sin will always either avoid talks regarding sex or talk against sex).

Suppression

This is with a clear motive and consciously avoiding the situation or feeling.

Intellectualization

This uses reasoning like rationalization. Most people who are involved in social and interpersonal work use this defence mechanism to remain in their work at the same time not accepting the flattering view of others. This defence mechanism separates the emotional and cognitive parts of an issue during handling.

Sublimation

- This is the highest form of defence.
- This is mostly a redirection of one impulse [usually sexual – (libido)] to another socially accepted activity – [writing a novel].
- As Freud believed most of our cultural life like music, drama, art is the defence of sublimation.
- This is a mature defence.
- Only those can use this defence whose sexual urges are at least partially fulfilled.

Note:

Defence mechanisms do not solve the actual problem. They only reduce the anxiety arising because of the problem.

Forming And Maintaining Rapport

Rapport in clinical practice is the relationship and understanding between the therapist and the client. The aim of this is for a change.

The change, here during the process of counselling and psychotherapy is made within the client/patient.

Psychotherapy – Greek work meaning – "Healing the soul" within the person – is an intrapsychic process.

How to work on Rapport?

1.   Identify an emotional problem.

     - Be specific towards the problem (the emotional content) of the client/patient.
     - Try to progress in your inquiry into the clients' underlying reasons for the emotional problem.
     - Deal each reasoning step by step which the client narrates.

2.   Ensure that the patient agrees to work with it.

     - Without the client's willingness for therapy it is unethical to start therapy.
     - You should find out what are the preventing factors of coming into therapy.

3.   Work on the conflict.
4.   Resolve the issue.
5.   Work on the conflict.

     - It is the patient's emotional suffering for which they seek help. The therapist should explore the defences, which make the client ignore the active situation and create intrapsychic conflict.
     - Any emotional problem has got three components to deal with: (a) Feeling, (b) Anxiety (c) Defences.
     - As a therapist, you must make realize the patient that he should act against the defence and not allow him to continue to remain in the psyche.
     - Forming a rapport and continuing therapy is to help the patient not to keep a distance from his symptoms, rather to resolve those.

6. Resolve the issue.

- This involves the entire process of therapy work.
    a. Know you are using defence. Know the type of defence you are using. Discard it.
    b. Hold on yourself to the situation and try to work with your apprehension and fear with the help of your therapist.
    c. Feel your emotional symptoms and change those to positive without using defences.
    d. Keep a motive to achieve the goal.

The patient sticks to a defence in one particular situation and finds a way to escape for a little situational peace, but if the internal agony still persists, it would get used up as a defence in other situations. So to remind the patient to quit the use of defences is the primary role of a therapist.

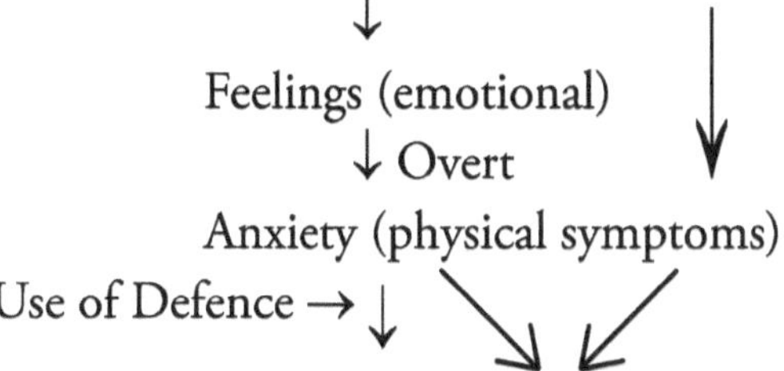

Apparently, the person function well but intra-psychic conflicts still remain.
So let go of the defences by therapy.

Example:-

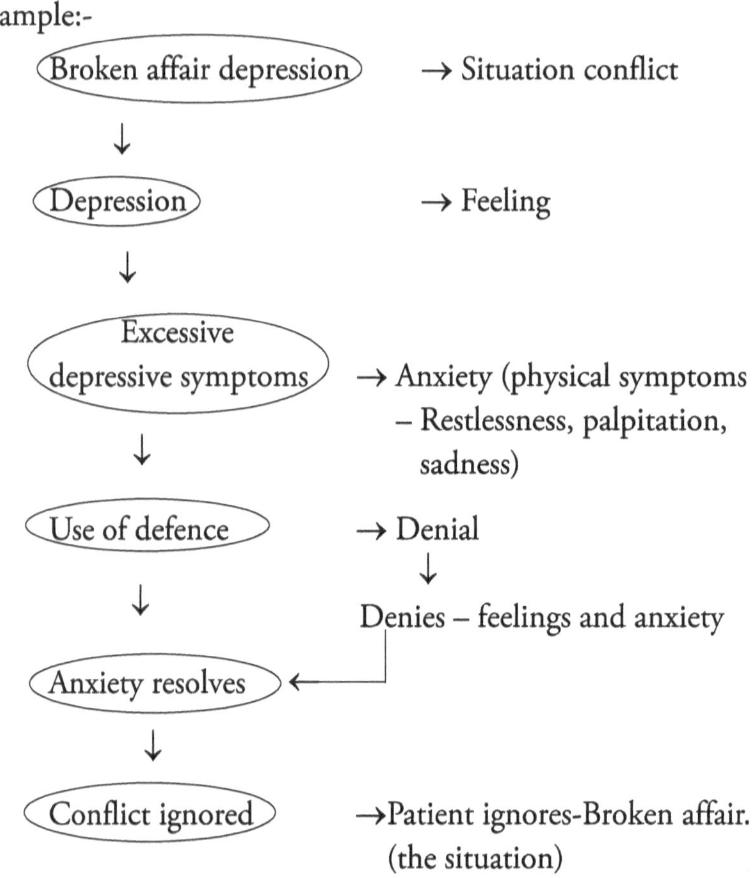

How to Go About the Therapy:

a. Tell the patient that we are in a process of working with feelings.

b. Tell the patient that defences are self-defeating.

c. Tell the patient that as a therapist I want to remove your psychological ailments for which you came.

d. Tell the patient to understand the anger, restlessness, and fear he is having.

e. Tell the patient to understand the symptoms both psychological and physical, he is having and not ignore those.

f. After understanding the therapeutic process is for his personal well-being he should be encouraged to find the way out of the shell of defences.

How to gain from therapy?

a. A clear awareness of the patient's own disarmament of psychic power by use of defence and its effects causing anxiety.

b. To reduce anxiety and to resolve the conflict.

c. To have a goal-directed mind.

What are the deterrents for therapeutic work and how to manage?

a. Not suggestible for working on with the therapist.

- Make the patient suggestible if he is a little unaware of his emotional content in a conflicting situation. This will create a consciousness of his feelings and the causes & effects of the conflict. Once the patient becomes consciously aware of his conflicting situation, the initial part of the therapy will become a little stressful for the patient and that is where the therapist works on to resolve the conflict and to help the patient to achieve his unconscious goal.

b. Hostility towards the therapist/therapeutic work.

- If the patient is hostile, try to make understand the patient and his problem. Involve him in therapy. Slowly and innovatively help the patient to reduce his anxiety.

If the patient is defiant then the therapist may tell the client to take a little pause and think over what to do about the therapy.

c. Not coming up with the actual problem.

Usually, the patients who do not come out of their problem easily, they use mature defences (example: Repression). Here the therapist should focus on a particular symptom and try to obstruct the defence continuously. Every time exploring the symptom and obstructing the defence, the therapist should tell the patient how much defences can harm you. By doing this the patient comes out of his problem.

If the patient having too many symptoms like anxiety, then help the patient to cool down, and then the therapist may proceed to explore the symptoms.

d.   Sometimes the patient uses defences like Rationalization, Denial, Projection, and Reaction formation which precipitates his symptoms. Different defence mechanisms will create different symptoms. So the therapist should explore the defences according to the symptoms. Mostly more symptomatic patients neglect unconsciously the events for which they suffer.

Once the patient comes out of his actual problem, he should aim for a positive outcome. If there is any obstacle in the patient's psyche that should be clearly discussed with the therapist. Sometimes because of chronic stress and depressive symptoms, the patient remains confused, hopeless, helpless, and worthless. These prevent him from a positive outcome.

e.   Not identifying the emotional problem.
f.   The emotional problem is presented as somatoform symptoms.

Even if the patient does not consciously identify his emotional feelings and sufferings, still he is slightly having a conflicting flicker of thoughts regarding the poor well-being of self. And for this, he constantly searches for self well-being although at a very instinctual/unconscious level. So the therapist should target this and formulate his way to probe and make the patient aware consciously that his emotional contents need to be consciously dealt with by him. This may take a few sessions and the therapist should remember there is a risk of developing dependency by the patient which should be handled. Secondly, as the patient's emotional contents are unconscious he is more likely to present somatic symptoms as anxiety.

The somatic symptoms can be released from the patient as anxiety resolution (see earlier notes how anxiety is dealt with).

Every human being how unconsciously he acts does not matter. The growing is to have "Original Freedom", to merge with the truth that may be too much potentiating to psychological trauma. This only needs a therapeutic conscious relationship with the therapist. This is truly a master, disciple relationship where sometimes the disciple should lead the master.

Symptoms from the Periphery to the Core

1.   External stimulus – Failure.
Tell the patient your current (emotional) feelings are different from what caused it (the external stimulus) and assist him till he differentiates between the two.

2.   Feelings (Emotional) – Sadness.
Tell the patient the emotional feeling is different than the Anxiety (the bodily response) and make the two apart and deal with these separately.

Example: The husband scolded wife and wife got afraid. This is a bodily feeling, the Anxiety. But the emotional feeling underlying is, the wife is angry.

Here the anger is encapsulated by fearfulness (being afraid). So deal with the anger first, and then the bodily feelings of being afraid will be resolved. Tell the patient that your anger is just a barrier to your underlying love for your partner, just remove it and see.

3.   Anxiety (bodily feelings) – Motor symptoms like muscle tension.
4.   Use of self Defence – There might be something wrong that caused this failure.

Once you tell the patient the anger is thought in response to the stimulus and keep aside it and then deal with the anxiety the bodily symptoms like muscle tension. The therapist should tell the patient to see the use of defence is restricting the actual result of the conflict (i.e. anxiety). Make the patient realize that the defence is out, then anxiety can be dealt with ease and the conflicts can be resolved. Always defence seriously hampers the ultimate living of the patient.

Neurotics always feel that their problem is because of others and this is because the patient does not know that this is due to his defences which hide the stimulus and suppresses the anxiety symptoms.

a. All ow the patient to realize the defences he is using.

b. Allow the patient to understand his bodily symptoms – the muscle tension which is because of the use of defences and those will not last long.

As the patient dogmatically thinks his bad time is because of his inability, failure or he is so bad that he deserves this and this creates Guilt.

The therapist's role is to allow the patient to realize that bad time does not last long and it is because you allow your defences to persist.

Core point – The end result – Guilt.

The patient is partially aware of these above factors.

To make the patient aware of all these factors from the periphery to core, the patient has to be explained all the above factors till he experiences his unconscious feelings. The patient should see and feel all the above five points sequentially and during the process, the therapist will intervene to help the patient to reassess his ability.

Once the patient reaches the core (guilt) from the periphery (stimulus), the therapist should tell the patient that there is a stimulus which generated the feelings and those were inappropriately dealt with because of the use of defences which created guilt and hence the patient should realize –

- Stimulus creates feelings.
- Feelings dealt with inappropriately by defences.
- This creates Psychopathological symptoms.

Defences Are Learnt Automatically

Defences are socially learnt and people express their feelings and show their behaviour with automatic use of defences. So people do not understand their behaviour is guided by defences. In stressful situations, these defences become more implicit and the behaviour becomes more stubborn. Most defences are ego symptomatic for which the patient does not feel stress and does not identify those and hence the core feelings are not identified.

Patients assume their own selves as their defences forgetting the stimulus and the feelings. As long as the patient is having ego symptomatic defences the conflict will remain intact.

To resolve the conflict and reduce the anxiety the therapist has to aware the patient about defences and tell him because of the defences he was having anxiety and that created all the pathological mental state.

Suicide Assessment and Prevention

Warning Signs

- All the warning signs are a cry for help.
- Death and terminal illness of any near and dears.
- Divorce, separation, broken relationship, loss of a job.
- Risk-taking behaviour.
- Depression.
- Adolescents around the age of 18 yrs face the first crisis phase, almost range up to depressive symptoms, suicidal ideas, and not properly diagnosed and properly treated. Hence they are very much vulnerable to committing suicide.
- Writing about death.
- Sudden mood changes: from outspoken to withdrawn and vice versa.
- Significant changes in daily activities.
- Changes in eating and sleeping habits.
- Searching for lethal objects.
- Making a will, – Unexpected phone calls and a visit to families and friends.

Common Statements People Give Who Experience Impending Suicidal Thoughts

- Feel very much sad.
- Everything is lost.
- Cannot see my future.
- Feel guilty – there is no way out.
- Feel helpless, hopeless, and worthless.

- Nobody is there to help.
- You will remember me when I am dead.
- You cannot stop me from dying.
- I do not want any help.

Common Ways to Help People Who Face Suicidal Ideas (suicide Prevention)

A. Counselling

- Tell this crisis phase comes to everyone's life sometimes or other and people manage it.
- This is a crisis and every crisis is temporary but death is permanent.
- Tell the person in crisis:

    - To speak regarding his feelings, talk freely.
    - To listen to others.
    - Join more friends and families.
    - There are alternatives in life. (Do not give glib reassurance)
    - Give support and also take assistance from other agencies for crisis intervention.
    - Discussing suicide openly may help the suicidal person to ameliorate his suicidal thoughts.

B. In campus mental health centre or special centres with mental health professionals for suicide prevention.

- Immediate contact with family members. If past history of medical treatment the doctor should be contacted.
- If there is any illness prior to being diagnosed or currently diagnosed should be treated as per medical advice.

Supportive therapy should be given at least for ameliorating depressive feelings and feelings of failure. Also, make the patient feel not alienated.

C. Talk to the suicidal person and only then the person might get an opportunity to express his/her thoughts and feelings. And that can provide him relief from his suicidal, negative, lonely, sad feelings. Ultimately this can prevent a suicide attempt.

- Start talking to the person in a very formal way like:

    - I am observing certain changes in your facial expression, emotion, and communication. Can you explain those?
    - I am concerned about you.
    - Since how long you are feeling like this?
    - Is there any big factor which is bothering you lately?
    - Please tell me how can I help you?
    - Tell the person who is suicidal that you are never alone here, we all are here with you.
    - When things will change definitely you will feel you did the right thing by seeking help.

- If anytime you feel it's enough I cannot hold it more, just tell you can just wait for a few minutes.
- Any negative feeling would be there, will all act positively for suicide. So ventilate.
- Tell suicidal thoughts are just temporary thoughts.

Do not have a discussion with the suicidal person:

- By blaming suicide as a sinful act, as that will make him feel like a sinful person.
- That will make his family more burdened, as he would retrieve that still, he is a burden to his family.

D. Quick action to prevent suicide:

In a suicidal patient:

1. Assess immediate threats.
2. Risks for committing suicide in the future. Assess – Impulses, Ideas, Plans, the timing of a future suicide attempt.

3. The severity of suicide plan – If severe, may have – Suicidal thoughts, plans (lethal), will persistently tell to commit suicide.
4. Keep objects away from the suicidal person which is lethal.
5. Always someone should accompany the suicidal person.

E. Empathetic Support:

- Let the suicidal person feel that you are there to support him. At the same time as helping a suicidal person itself can induce suicidal emotions in the helper, so he/she should take care of himself/herself.
- The person who is helping a suicidal person should:

1. Get some structured, professional help for the suicidal person.
2. Make sure the suicidal person to take treatment, maintain compliance, come for regular follow up.
3. He/she should be proactive to help the person who is suicidal as those people feel themselves outcasted.
4. Rehabilitate by lifestyle changes:
5. Food, exercise, music, sports, reading, meditation, yoga are a few areas to work on.
6. Ensure all safety with the person who is suicidal:

   - Crisis intervention, call centres phone number.
   - Doctors/Counsellors phone no.
   - Stopping all triggering substances.
   - To know how to take self-care.
   - Remove harmful objects from the access of the person.
   - If the person is on an antidepressant it is mandatory to observe for increase suicidal thoughts especially during the initial recovery phase when the person gets the energy to commit the act of suicide.

Suicidal Behaviour

- Self-inflicted injuries, – Risk-taking and reckless behaviour
- Repeated accidents, – Requests for euthanasia, – Morbid theme stories, – sudden ambiguous behaviour, – Psychotic state (Auditory Hallucination – Hearing some voices telling to commit suicide).

Suicide Rating Scales

1. Suicide probability scale (Cull & Gill – 1992).
2. Beck scale for suicide Ideation (Beck).
3. Suicidal Ideation Questionnaire (Reynold).

Mental Status Examination for Suicidal Patients/clients

- MSE is usually done to describe the patient/client's level of self acquisition, presentation, and functioning.
- Usually, the MSE is done around the following aspects:

  - Appearance, attitude
  - Attribution
  - Mood, affect
  - Speech
  - Thought – process, content, perception
  - Cognition, judgement (crude & fine)
  - Insight

Grief Reaction: Working Through Counselling

Grief Reaction

Grief can take you to the forgotten truth. The moment of the present is the moment to be in. To remain in the present is to be with the truth. Consciously or unconsciously we are always at the present and hence with the truth. Grief and pain make us conditioned to let go of our pain and go nearer to the truth. Unless otherwise we feel the pain and know the art of releasing it, there can not be any change. As we surpass pain with a complete consciousness we attain the truth.

Grief is an emotional reaction that people undergo during different phases of life. Most of those are like – Death impending for self, Death of a near and dear, Broken affair, Financial loss, Shifting of family members to other places.

The healing of grief reaction starts from mourning and the healing process is very gradual. It needs different types of counselling. The simplest therapy considered is supportive therapy.

If the death of an individual is suffering from a terminal illness, people can make up their mind and the intensity of grief becomes low. If one dies suddenly we may feel guilty. With a sudden loss of a near relative or very close one then he may blame himself that probably he could have done something to stop his death.

Death or any other significant reason for which grief starts, it shows few symptoms like: All patterns of sleep are disturbed, overeating or loss of appetite, headache, excessive urination, and bowel frequency, body pain, sadness, lethargic feelings, social withdrawal fatigue, suicidal ideas.

Coping with Grief (due to Death and Other Losses)

Every individual has got a different attitude, attributes, and personality. They react differently to different stressful situations and the coping mechanism is very much personalized towards grief and stress.

Some individuals when face death of some near ones or loss which is significant to produce stress, they try to find out a solution for the same with the help of others and try to find the same past good memories. They also try to make themselves busy in some activities. Few people of the grief reaction go into depression, show social withdrawal and hopeless, helpless, and worthless feelings for the world and self.

For some people, a professional counsellor/therapist may do in a better way to resolve their grief. Most of us forget that a child can be the one who is most vulnerable to the death of a loved one and think of them as no grievers. Very young kids even around the age of six months or thereafter start grieving if they go through a phase of especially parental loss (more of a maternal loss) as they provide contact comfort to them.

Another fact is that a child can be a double folded griever if one parent dies. Because if one parent dies the other parent grieves and goes through a serious depressive phase and hence the child grieves for – the loss of the parent and – the psychological/depressive phase of the surviving parent.

Here it requires specialized counselling for both the child and the surviving parent for crisis intervention and further grief resolution. The most important thing to alleviate the grief of a sibling loss like the death of one parent is that society to come around and support him.

* Grief reaction of a child is entirely different than adults. The child might not talk, cry, or show much of emotional expression. But the psychological trauma, the child goes through is almost very difficult to manage. So the counsellors should give utmost importance to this. The most helpful would be making contact with a bereavement group.

Stages of Grief Reaction (Especially due to death, Terminal illness)

(a) Denial, (b) Discussion, (c) Negotiation, (d) Depression and (e) Acceptance.

Identifying the stages helps a counsellor to set up a working module with the client. The counsellor once identifies the emotional attributions, feelings of the client can use the technical ways to counsel in that particular stage. Different individuals have different ways of coping. So at one particular stage, different individuals may need different types, ways, and intensity of counselling.

Meaning to the Stages of Grief/Death

a. Denial – The person at first denies or does not accept the reason for the grief.
b. Discussion – What/how the cause happened.
c. Negotiation – The person negotiates to defy or decrease the intensity of the reason.
d. Depression – The result of acute impending stress which does not have an axis to rotate.
e. Acceptance of the happenings all around.

Grief is experienced suddenly and mostly without giving an alarm. With appropriate support, the intensity of grief reduces over time. When grief takes its form different types of emotional responses are evident like hopeless and helpless feelings. Strong preoccupation with the events makes the person confused and depressive thought ruminations persist. All these can be taken care of by an expert counsellor.

Self-Help Ways

The victim of grief can find ways of self-help by:

- Talking to family and friends.
- Contacting a counsellor, – Joining NGOs.
- Looking for specific self-help groups.
- Regularizing the daily routines.

- Taking proper care of physical health.
- Listening to music, doing relaxation/meditation (if appropriate).
- Maintaining reading habits.
- Communication.
- Talking to other people who in past have suffered from grief.
- Faith in Almighty.
- Adequate sleep is required.

Finally consult a psychiatrist, counsellor, or psychotherapist for guiding the future plans. Many people who go through a period of grief try to reduce the same by using addictive substances, avoiding socialization, stopping going to work, not expressing the difficulties he/she is facing.

Grief Reaction And Coping During Childhood

(Age Up to Adolescence)

Early Childhood: Death appears as a sudden loss, shock, creates significant confusion. Sometimes the child stops talking and eating. But this intense response is for a short period of only a few days (very brief in duration) and the child comes back to normalcy with the support of other caregivers. It is usually reversible. Gross situational effects are seen – Example – If a father dies the child shows symptoms of what the father was fulfilling. Usually, a father substitute decreases all these effects. * The child would seek to know about the event repeatedly and how it happened.

* Once the superego starts developing around the age group of 8 years change the child's concept of death and grief. Here the child may start realizing death is irreversible and there is a permanent loss. * The child perceives the future as difficult because of the loss of a significant figure in his/her life. * The child may take the help of other significant figures in his/her life to compensate for the grief.

Around the preadolescent, to adolescent age, the child can make some finer thinking of death and its meaning. Here the responses to grief reaction would be like: (1) Sudden psychological shock, (2) Sadness, (3) Denial of the event, (4) Anger, (5) Realization, Rationalization, and Regression, (6) Acceptance of the event.

Counselling Needs for a Child Who Suffer Grief

A young child around ego developing period:

- Talk to the child very calmly, considerately.
- Act like long-term support.
- Encourage to talk regarding his/her emotions.
- Engage the child in some constructive work.
- Repeated reassurance of help.
- As the child around the age of 8 years can have a judgemental capacity the child should be explained clearly regarding the event not lying anything. During this age group, the child is also explained about the rituals of death. Not only the counsellor is involved in the process but family members also should be advised to be involved in the process.

The emotional needs of the child have to be fulfilled.

Counselling Needs for a Child Who Suffer Grief

Adolescent:

Expresses grief instantly but the same come to reality soon. When they suffer from grief for a long time the counsellor should:

- Make him a part of the planning for the future.
- Try to make him learn to do some decision makings.
- He should be informed about rituals and ceremonies and should give him the confidence to become a leader.
- The counsellor should guide him

    - How to maintain all social relations.

- How to observe and learn from his friends who are in a similar situation.
- To express his emotions, future plans.

Few Things Which Need Attention

- The counsellor should keep in mind that any special occasions like anniversaries (Death, Marriage, others), birthdays, family, and social functions; holidays are a vulnerable period for the grief victim. So extra efforts should be given to the victim to support, counsel, and guide him.
- The grief victims express their unconscious or subconscious emotions in their activities. So, those should be given appropriate direction.
- You should express your genuine sorry feelings for the client's loss.
- Never give a false statement to the victim (especially regarding the loss. Also do not ask direct questions to the child regarding the event).
- If the person/child is in severe psychological distress (grief) because of an event, like death/serious loss do not try to give any direct suggestions like: "No one can change the destiny", or "Everything will be ok in course of time."

Activities for Grief Victims

- Communicating their problem associated with death or any cause of grief to the counsellor, family members, friends, social workers, community members, and NGOs.
- Working through grief.
- Interacting with family and group activities.
- Giving routine time to job, family, or if a student, to education.
- Involvement with peer groups.
- Interacting with a group in which many other people/children suffer from grief. Especially children should share their own problems

with others and feel others' problems and by doing this they get good psychological support to reassess and rebuild their present and future. There are different types of groups where the victims especially children can join like –

- Random groups.
- Small and structured groups.
- Mass interaction groups.
- Open-ended groups.
- Close-ended groups.
- Fixed session groups.
- Brief therapy groups.

Bereaved People Who Need Active Intervention

- If the person does not show any emotional expression immediately after the death/loss.
- If tells nothing major occurred.
- If a significant phobic reaction occurs off & on.
- If for any reason after death there occurs academic failure.
- Frequent place changes. Job changes also need immediate care.
- Drug and Alcohol abuse. Grossly decreased Appetite or overeating.
- If the person develops suicidal depression or very impulsive behaviour and also significant disturbance in sleep.
- If the person shows gross marital coping disturbance.
- If shows socially deranged behaviour.
- If the person shows sudden cruelty towards the pets and other animals.
- Significant social withdrawal.
- Lastly, if the event of death/other events with the same intensity are not told to the person for a long time, then when he will come to know, might create unmanageable circumstances and hence needs active intervention by the therapist.

Existential Counselling and Happiness

Considering the topics like Death, God, and Existence were when we as counsellors discuss the above topic consciously and subconsciously follow Existential counselling in some way. Prominent existential theorists are Kierkegaard, Nietzsche, Husserl, and others. (1) According to this theory, one of the explanations is 'the sickness unto death.' People suffer from ill-defined guilt and accept death as truth. Kierkegaard wrote that truth could only be found by being, not from thinking and that the element most lacking in people was the courage to live with passion and commitments from the inner depths of their being.

(2) According to another theory by Friedrich Nietzsche is that the basis of human self-affirmation was 'God is dead.' He perceived that individuals are always in the quest for a new. This brings the power to live and the sluggish to die. (3) Husserl's theory was – dualistic approach is wrong. Things needed to be described and understood but not analyzed and explained. (4) Jean-Paul Sartre (1905-80) also explained in his theory that the essence of human beings' existence is because of their struggle against the odds of life.

Life's only principle is to be happy and your happiness to decide your job of action. Your happiness should be in your way. Do not consider other's happiness and the way they get. People mostly choose to remain unhappy unconsciously and psychologically there are profound reasons for it. Psychologically, a social learning behaviour becomes most critical of giving happiness/unhappiness to the child.

If a child is unhappy and his surroundings are empathetic to him, give affection to him, he will generate love for others. When people give attention to a child, it acts like nourishment to the ego of the child, and the desire for happiness increases. Every child acts miserably to get attention, to become happier later. This is the real politics of life and it starts very early from infancy. At the same time, you are grown up and you seem happy towards others even if they act dubiously. So now you have to learn how to maintain your happiness.

If you are euphoric and enjoying your life, people will try to prove you wrong. But if you are melancholic nobody will think the same which is happening to you from the very core of your heart. The entire society is based on misery and your ecstasy will make the society perturbed. But do not worry; you go on your own way for happiness and that is the real way of living life. If you are blissful and happy, you cannot go for nonsense arguments.

If you are happy there will never be an unrealistic urge of hoarding money and this will ameliorate your entire life.

The entire society lives in misery and this is why every child first learns to become miserable. To stay in misery is your lifetime investment. So you choose to be in misery. On the contrary, to be in a happy state of mind is easier than to be in misery.

Every society makes miserable people out of joyful creators. Every child by birth is smiling, happy. But during death, he is just psychotic and this is the gift of our fellow societal members.

A child, to begin with, is happy and everyone should try to regain their own childhood ego. When a child becomes unhappy or angry he becomes totally involved in it and his entire being, the entire energy becomes his act and the child remains the same beautiful child. He seems even more beautiful. There remains no conflict after he becomes silent and his ego function is supported.

The principle is if you merge with any type of emotion you become the same. You are just a blissful one and hence you are not satisfying your ego functions, you are unhappy. So be one with your ego. To be intensely involved with the present is eternal and then there will be a continuous flow of happiness.

Life is yours, the play of life is yours and you are the actor. So play with wisdom. Do not ask for happiness from any Guru, Master, or well-wisher. **If you create your misery, you can create your happiness.**

Another principle to be happy is, make the ego "to let go." People make others learn to fight with ego and this is why they suffer. Truths can never be obtained by fighting with ego and for ages, this has been an utter ignorance.

To remove your sufferings go with your present, your ego. Existence is never an obstacle for you. The existence, nature is your mother. She feeds you with all odds and hence she cannot be your enemy. Moreover, you are just an atom. You cannot fight with the entire existence. So be in love with existence.

For happiness you do not have to quit anything, rather you have to understand it, and then you will be always with eternity. There have been many studies (psycho-physiological) regarding **contact comfort** and these show when a child is away from the mother or a mother substitute the child becomes irritable and physically weak. So it is ever true for everybody that Mother Nature cannot be against you. If you quit something from nature, you are the one to suffer. So go with your body, mind, existence, and a labile ego.

Most of us remain unhappy when we remember our past happy days during a stressful time.

Note: Whatever may be the situation around you, do not lose your hope for future good times. Think about your stress, seek advice from your well-wishers, accept all the happenings, and act positively.

Your unhappiness is your creation. Accept it. You will find the land of joy soon.

The best way to remain away from unhappiness is to stop thinking about happiness. You will discover yourself the next moment winning the game. Once you discover yourself you would be the happiest person.

People remain unhappy thinking about others. If they eliminate the thoughts of those insignificant others they may bring happiness into their life. Think about your own self, somewhere you will find happiness.

✱ ✱ ✱

When all thoughts evaporate happiness comes. Suspicion and doubts of the mind create unhappiness.

Comforts cannot measure happiness. Happiness is the ultimate comfort.

You are unhappy because you always console your mind that, unhappiness cannot come to you.

✱ ✱ ✱

Effects of Action

3 effects of action:

1. Effect – External to you.
2. Effect – Internal to you – Generosity, helpfulness, and kindness became your nature.
3. Effect – Cosmic – You will receive help in time of need.

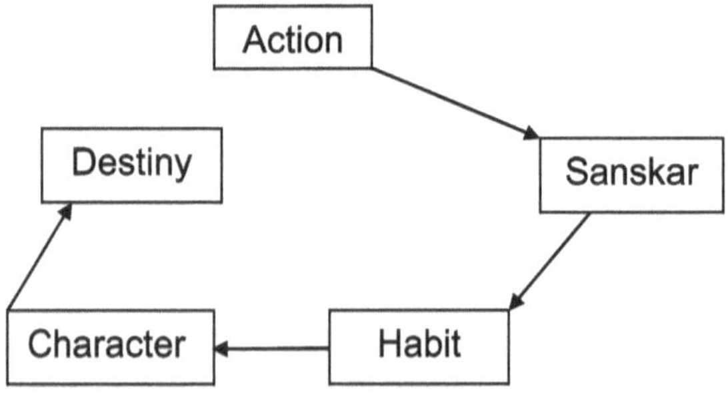

Sadness is mostly because of a fear of the loss of a loved object. Abraham – Freud's theory: If there is a loss of a loved object, you feel your loved body part is lost and become handicapped. So the feeling of the loss gives a depressing feeling.

Counselling a client who has suffered a distressing loss, I always talk about spiritual contexts from Bhagavad Gita. It refers to the concepts of (1) Detachment from the worldly elements and controlling five senses. (2) Meditation to calm the restless thoughts and to sustain attention to progress through happiness. (3) Controlling (mind) thoughts and behaviour through spiritual practices.

"antavanta ime deha
nijtyasyoktah saririnah
anasino prameyasya
tasmad yudhyasva bharata" → *Bhagavad Gita*

The above text implies that "The body and all the materials of the world will perish one day."

Worries are the biggest enemies of humans. Keep an arm's length from those and spread the seeds of contentment in your mind and generate passion for heaven and your worries would be replaced by wisdom.

A man is peaceful because of his latent abilities and is happy for his present.

Note: Insight-oriented therapy can be made a little easier with these words and making soothing interaction with clients.

It is a futile endeavour when a human being keeps faith in idols and tries to get happiness from the grace of God.

These faiths are rationalized behaviour, used as a psychological defence mechanism and this should be explained to the client that he/she is using rationalization as psychological defence and should come out of this and conquer fear which is an overt illusion to stress.

Neurochemical Correlates of Happiness

1. Dopamine
2. Serotonin
3. Oxytocin
4. Endorphins

Note: The above suggestions are to keep yourself realized about life and death and to be away from the worldly illusions so that you can have a meditative mind.

New You

You are the creator of your own destiny

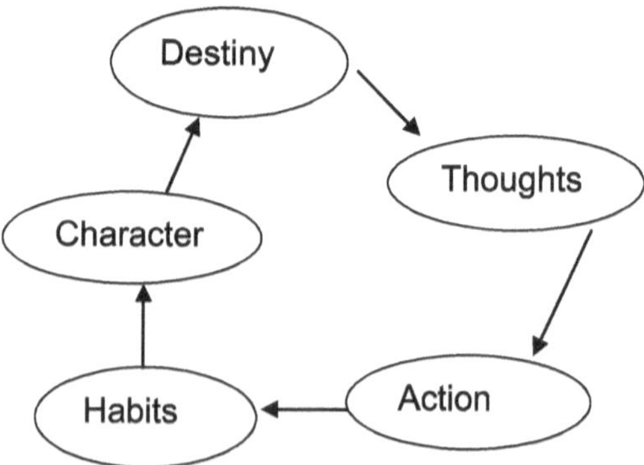

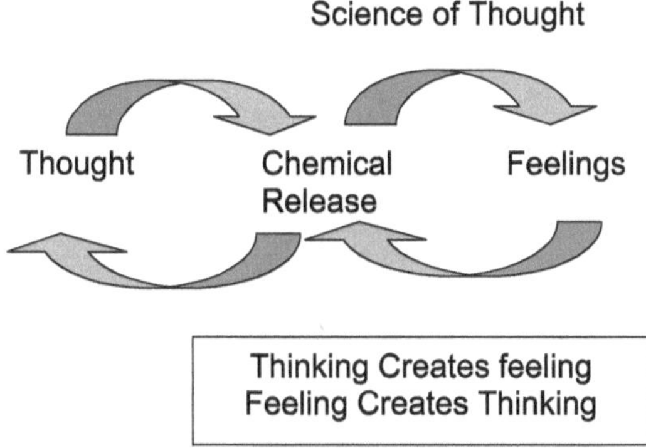

- There are four faculties of Mind:
    1. Manas
    2. Budhi
    3. Chitta
    4. Ahankar

Thoughts, Attitudes, Personalities

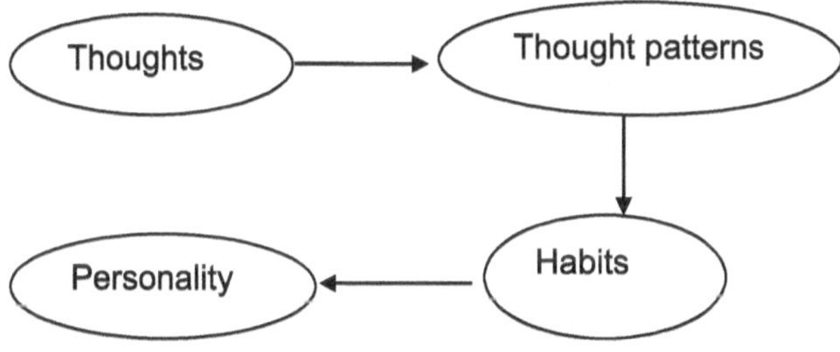

Mind management → Reversing the negative Bias

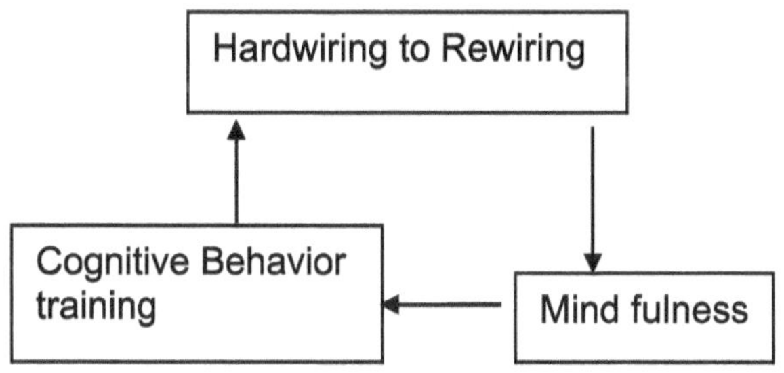

Cognitive Behaviour Training

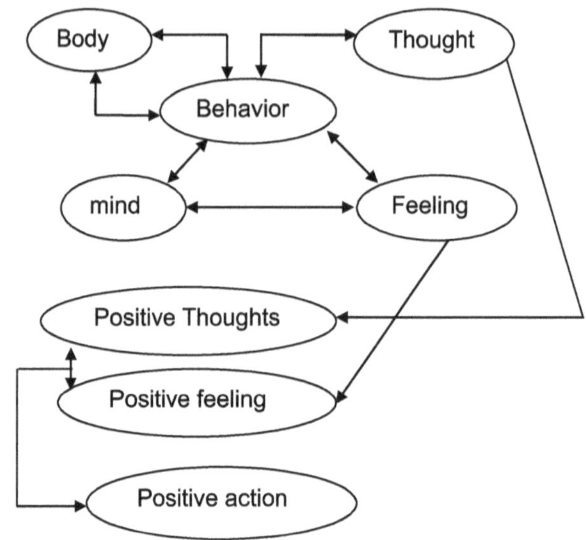

Mindfulness:

- Present moment
- Paying attention
- Non-Judgemental
- What you practice becomes stronger
- Mind and Body at one place
- Resilience
- Increased will power
- Understand emotions through cognition
- Ability to make decisions with clarity
- Mastery over our feeling

Kinder you, Gentler you.

> "If you centre yourself in nonbeing
> Your mind becomes one."

The Pursuit of Happiness

- The Philosophy of Upanishads is vedant.

- The Purpose of vedant is complete cessation of sorrow. The attainment of ultimate bliss.
- Something is true if it is useful.
- We are the children of immortal bliss.
- If you realize the immortal bliss you go beyond death.

Happiness – (p) Pleasure – transitory, diminishing, Habit-forming.

If you single-mindedly seek pleasure, Very soon you will find pleasure does not give pleasure.

- (E) Engagement
- (M) meaning – Higher goals

Five goals of Happiness

1. Spirituality > – Unselfishness
                      – Love the God
2. Pleasure
3. Possessions
4. Bliss
5. Liberation

The happiness we are chasing all through our life is within us. This happiness we get if our mind is calm, serene, and desireless.

Ways for Happiness

- Unselfish work   – Karma Yoga
- Love of God   – Bhakti Yoga
- The silence of mind – Raj Yoga (meditation)
- Divinity within us   – Existence
                          Consciousness } Gyan Yoga
                          Bliss

3 Purpose of Happiness in life:
- Self-confidence
- Goal in life
- Power of concentration

Happiness

- The purpose of vedant is "Atyantic Dukh Nibriti"
  i.e. – "Complete seizing of sorrow"
- " Paramanand Praptischa" – Attainment of ultimate bliss."

The goal of life: Dharma – Spirituality – Meaning (M)

  - Artha – Possessions – Engagement (E)
  - Kama – Pleasure (P)
  - Moukshya – Spiritual liberation

Logo Therapy

- This therapy is very much meaningful for life.
- This concept of counselling/psychotherapy was given by Victor Frankle. He was a follower of Freud and Adler. Initially, this concept was introduced to prisoners who were depressed and lost their hope in life (the meaning of life).
- Logo – a – Greek word – means – Meaning and spirit.
- Human beings seek always the meaning of life. This is the basis of Logotherapy.
- The theme of therapy – "By helping others I see the meaning of life and see a meaning in their life."

Assumptions of Therapy

- Life is short and full of possibilities. It is our endeavour to find the potentialities and quit the nonpossibilities.
- When people rise above their bodily and psychic dimensions it is called the "zoological" dimension.
- The main motivational force of human beings is to find the meaning of life which is the basic theory of Logotherapy. According to this therapy, the highest aim of life is to find its meaning, not self-actualization which is just a byproduct.

Logo therapy focuses on human beings' spiritual existence. It is based on the mind's consciousness which is awareness of self and thus the meaning of life can be discovered. Unconsciousness is (i) Spiritual and (ii) Instinctual.

- Existence exists in action rather than reflection – Frankle (1975)
- Logotherapy explains – (1) In everybody, in everything there remain everything at least in a latent stage. This is one important aspect of counselling. (2) Human being always transcends even if it is unconscious. (3) Human association with God is hidden and or God is hidden. We chose religiosity as one of our qualities without knowing our unconscious religious existentialism which causes neurosis.
- Conscience: As Frankle stated it is our ethical instinct and it acts like a trans-human agent. It is the religious voice of a human being.

Meaning of Life and Death

Accepting responsibilities and understanding the potentials within us to achieve future probabilities. In analytic counselling therapy often going into the past experiences and getting meaning of it can help for making a meaningful present.

Quality of death gives quality to life. We should know and act on our responsibilities every time so that we can get the meaning of life.

We should know our inner freedom of spirituality, eternity which can take us beyond our destiny.

Many mystics especially of Asian origin they tell to search the self. But the basic need of a human being in this life is to search for the meaning of life which can give us the identity. Today, people are only concern about their own desires forgetting their inner selves. Frankle says those who do not get meaning in their life they suffer from neurotic problems. Human sufferings have got a strong root as they do not actually know what they want to do and hence depend on two things – (1) Confirmation (following other activities). (2) Totalitarianism (following the instructions of others). These two things are a deterrent to getting meaningfulness in life.

Meaninglessness in life is perceived because of:

1. Disruption in traditional values.
2. The belief in their values of life is already determined.
3. Difficulty in finding a good counsellor, a role model.

In Logotherapy, the clients are counselled and guided for finding their own meaning of life. When the client will tell his life does not have any meaning only then he can be guided towards meaningfulness and to be assured that this disparity is not a symptom. Tell the client this is an intellectual growth.

Imagine life is a series of moving pictures that are currently being filmed.

Tell the clients to complete their work with a limited time but the deadline is not confirmed.

Spirituality and mental health facts:

1. It increases the coping mechanism by giving values like – respect, – faith, hope, interaction.
2. It creates the values of social communication, service to people.
3. Participation in religious activities gives a celestial, serenity to life.
4. It gives confidence in work and positive thinking.
5. Provides a good mental state.

Meditation Therapy

Requirements For Meditation

1. Regular
2. Fixed time
3. Place – Fixed
4. Mat (Asana)
5. Do not struggle with unpleasant thoughts
6. Concentration on a particular point
7. Changing the association which disturbs you
8. Company
9. The practice of simplicity – asceticism
10. Possession
11. Attitude
12. Detachment
13. Go to meditation with the feeling of eternity
14. Yearning for God/truth
15. Trying to connect your day to day activities to God
16. Meet spiritual people (Power of holy company)

There is no like or dislike in me, no greed or delusion
      I know not pride or jealousy
I have no duty, no desire for wealth, lust, or liberation
I am the form of consciousness and bliss
I am the eternal Shiva …

I have no fear of death, no caste or creed
I have no father, no mother, for I was never born
I am not a relative, nor a friend, nor a teacher nor a learner

I am the form of consciousness and bliss
I am the eternal Shiva …

I am devoid of duality, my form is formless
I exist everywhere pervading all senses
I am neither attached, nor free or captive
I am the form of consciousness and bliss
I am the eternal Shiva …

I am not virtue or vice, nor pleasure or pain
I need no mantras, no pilgrimage, no scriptures or rituals,
I am not the experienced, nor the experience itself
I am the form of consciousness and bliss
I am the eternal Shiva …

I am not the mind, the intellect, the ego, or the memory,
I am not the ears, the skin, the nose, or the eyes
I am not space, not earth not fire, water, or wind
I am the form of consciousness and bliss
I am the eternal Shiva …

I am not the breath, nor the five elements
I am not matter nor the five sheaths of consciousness
nor I am the speech, the hands, or the feet
I am the form of consciousness and bliss
I am the eternal Shiva …

– Adi Shankaracharya

Dealing With Disturbance During Meditation

When disturbances come, do you know you are disturbed?

Yes.

That one who knows you are disturbed is not disturbed. The knower of the disturbance is not disturbed. Because it was present before the disturbance came and it will be present after the disturbance is gone.

The disturbance is recognized in your light and it is resolved in your light. But that light is free of disturbance so you are free of disturbance. When the disturbance was there you the awareness was not disturbed. Even if disturbance comes you should know you are the undisturbed Brahman. You are that ever pure unchanging consciousness.

- Meditation is silence, a thoughtless mind. It is the pure consciousness the absolute supremacy over the mind. The consciousness when stands alone and there remains no thought only the consciousness and at that moment you will feel you do not stand anywhere only the Almighty everywhere.
- Meditation is not philosophy, it is a science. It is not a laboratory but still, it is a science. For meditation only requirement is your motivation.
- Meditation takes you beyond the mind and alleviates sadness, gives youthfulness and peace.
- Forgoing into meditation do not think over it. Because thinking creates thoughts that deprive meditation. Mind's function is to think and if you become aware of yourself there will be the death of mind and then meditation starts.

Is meditation fake?

Telling, instructing, and guiding for meditation is fake. You do anything it just becomes an act with an underlying thought/idea. No thought, no idea can go up to meditation. When you become only an observer of your own vital functions (involuntary) you can achieve the state of meditation. And this means peace, life, and death.

* In meditation miseries and happiness vanish. What remains is peace.

* No one can enter into meditation just for the sake of knowing it.

* Either put all your energy to jump into meditation (dynamic meditation) forget entirely the source of your life energy, then you can enter into meditation – "Osho".

"The 'Dhyana' gate is like an alabaster vase, white and transparent; within their burns steady golden fire, the flame prajna, that radiates from Atma."

H. P. Blavatsky.

Meditation as a part of psychological therapies in the U.S. is having a high proportion of all therapies including medical. According to a study in the U.S. is around 10% of psychological therapies are meditational practices in its different variants.

Meditation is practised in different parts of the world based on religious, cultural aspects.

Meditation is:

- No mind, no thought state
- It is not concentration; rather it is just opposite to it.

Meditation allows our stored energy to flow either upwards or downwards. It brings an inner-self awareness.

If all these can happen the miseries, anxiety, depression, apprehension will go out.

It solves the highest purpose of life. Once you are in a meditational process all your labile emotions, aggression, disgust will be washed out.

Few simple principles of meditation:

- To start meditation, use your mind to feel the nature/existence around you even though you are in a meditation hall. Reduce your thoughts. Make your body (muscles) and mind relaxed.
- As meditation will ascend you will be in a no-mind state.

The basic requirement for meditation:

- To remain close to nature
- Maintain silence
- Clothes that make one feel comfortable.
- Meditational music.

Basic Facts of Meditation

- It does the relaxation of body muscles.
- Increase lung volume and oxygenation in the brain.
- Start with cognitive imagery.
- Breaking psychological defence mechanisms.
- Focusing on target areas of the body differently for different types of meditations.
- Meditation increases mental stability, physical functions, and improves the body's immunity to fight illnesses.
- It increases the spiritual healing power and release of endorphins which take care of the cardiovascular system and other physical ailments.

Long-term practice of meditation once a day (30-45 minutes) can give positive results like:

- Reduces blood pressure (to normal).
- Normalize cardiac function.
- Oxygenation of the brain is improved thus increasing memory and thought functions.
- Normalizes digestive functions.
- Reduces the risks of psychological illnesses like anxiety, depression, and high emotional labiality.
- Neurobiological changes show changes in blood circulation or metabolism which give positive health.

To meditate is the quest, to seek, to search. What to search? Definitely, it is happiness, peace, eternity, and Almighty. But this seeking is the first step after which the meaning of seeking becomes antagonistic to meditation.

Why meditate?

To release stress.

In meditation, we search for an understanding of our inner morality but not social morality which may be totally disordered.

Meditation is bringing the mind to stability, orderly without any conscious demand on it. The mind is always at a conflict. These conflicts should be resolved in harmony with the external situation (conflict resolution). Mind at no stage can resolve conflicts with efforts. Because any effort is a stressful factor for the individual. This creates more intense conflicts. So it has to be understood that no forceful effort, no forceful orderliness is required for meditation. At any stage of a meditative process, there should not be a duality of mental activity.

Note

A very important psychological process known as crisis intervention or resolution is psychological distress which needs counselling and moves over meditation would give a much better output.

> "Do not fool yourself with all the books written about
> meditation, or with all people who tell you how to meditate,
> or the groups that are formed in order to meditate. For
> if there is no order, which is a virtue, the mind must live
> in the efforts of contradictions. How can such a mind
> be aware of the whole implication of meditation?"
>
> **– J. Krishnamurti**

The only answer to meditation is to be silent like a bird sitting over a tree and no mind action should be there.

The second factor to start meditation is to love and this love is not for pleasure, pain, or piety. This is only to observe your life.

Dreams are the mind games of all-day-long activities. When you closely observe all these activities you probably do not have a dream and hence you cannot do meditation in dreams as dreams are observing the past activities in the subconscious mind and meditation is just a state of mind where no thought is present.

The difference between the experience in meditation and experience with drug effect (many Indian so-called Yogis and Tantriks take drugs for supernatural experience) is that in meditation the observer and the observation become one there remains no gap. But with the effects of drugs people observe certain things but the gap between the observer and observation is big and it is a very short-lasting delusional perception or an impact of hallucinogens.

Few worship a statue, few go for meditation. The beginning is beyond both.

Silence speaks the highest truths and lies and this is meditation. Meditation gives you the ultimate price in life.

Life and death never mean different. Both present deep in life and death. So the panic thoughts regarding life events should be eradicated from the mind with meditation.

Note

The meditational process starts with mindfulness but meditation occurs when one attains complete silence in the mind and then he can experience the truths of life.

Types of meditation you can follow

Anapani Sati Yog Dhyan, Bipasana, and Yoga Nidra Dhyan, and many other types may be followed.

Spirituality is the process of self-knowing. Knowing self is putting the mind completely into existence and once that happens you are as solitary as the Almighty.

Everyone is having a temple within. So pray within.

Wind makes the ocean turbulent and the sailor stops sailing. When the ocean is calm the wind takes its part. You be calm, time will take you to the Almighty; (The Bhagabat Gita Way).

Note:
The above quotations mean, be silent and calm your nerves, look at your inner-self and you can go up to self-actualization. The meditation you can follow: Kundalini, Chakra Dhyan (Osho), Sabasana, etc.

Spirituality is the path of self-knowledge and going to the zero-dimensional aspects of human life.

Every act somehow or other is debatable. The state of no thought, no act is eternal (meditation).

When something unusual starts repeatedly for sometimes, it creates an awareness of divinity and peace.

Meditation is the way to conquer death.

Meditation begins with creativity.

Note:
The mind should be alone in the path of meditation. It should not be burdened by any exterior objects. Meditation can reach

you at its highest point only through your own insight. And the entire process of reaching to insight should contain no dual thought, only acceptance.

Salient Benefits of Spirituality and Meditation

1. It gives cortisol and other hormonal appropriate levels which reduces the bodily response to acute stress.
2. Positive thinking produces a 30 per cent drop in the perception of pain.
3. Progress of dementia and Alzheimer's disease becomes slow.
4. Regular participation in religious activities lowers mortality by 12 per cent a year.
5. People who undergo cardiac rehabilitation they get more improvement than non-religious participants.
6. Reduce the dependency on drug addiction and other psychological ailments.
7. Spirituality increases the relaxation response of the body and decreases the body's response to stress.
8. Meditation improves the immune functions of the body and improves the WBC counts.
9. Prayer is friendly to heart and mind.
10. Positive thinking in ICU gives better results.

Spirituality is what brings you peace and safety. It can be achieved through God-worshipping, nature-liking, meditation, yoga, chanting mantras, doing deep muscle relaxation, etc.

Features of Spiritual Awakening:

1. A tendency to let things happen rather than make them happen.
2. More smiling and cheerful than ever.
3. Feelings of being connected with others and nature.
4. Appreciation of other's activities.

5.   Thinking and acting spontaneously rather than from fear or past experience.
6.   Ability to enjoy everything.
7.   Not worrying about things that used to happen earlier.
8.   Not interested in other activities.
9.   Gaining the power to love self and others.
10.   Not confronting others.

Counselling for Aggressive/Impulsive Behaviour

De-Stress Your Self By Controlling Aggression

Anger and impulses are just like flashing and lightning, which indicates you should be cared for in a safe place at an appropriate time.

If you are irritable, aggressive, and showing impulsive behaviour, you can control those on your own by following a few simple steps:

1. Your mental state should be aware of your behaviour.
2. Quit impulsive external behaviour.
3. Find out the cause of your aggressive and impulsive mental state.
4. Take a pause, so that you can control your thoughts and behaviour (both internal and external aggressive behaviour).
5. Find out the ways by which your anger can be controlled, resolved smoothly.
6. Whatever may be the situation your action should be positive and constructive.

Use your psychological defence mechanisms throughout the process of resolving anger like:

- Rationalization
- Displacement.
- Sublimation (here the person uses substitute activity to replace a frustrating behaviour into constructive and artistic work).

Anger, impulsiveness is not wholesome of your life. It is just an episodic event and thinks that every event is short-lived and you can change your behaviour the next moment.

- Talk to yourself both silently and with a loud voice regarding your impulses by which you'll be conscious about what you are going to do and this will restrain your apparent downfall.
- If you feel your offender is wrong, just tell him the other way, he would be right.
- Any provocation you face, deal with a little smile to the other, or just take the other road to your house.
- The best way to release your negative energy and angry bits, just tell God please forgive me for my ignorance.

Most of our aggressive impulses/behaviours are either of a valid reason or the one which is not valid.

The valid impulses, for example, you have been betrayed and for which you are angry and showing some impulsivity, can be perceived as all the God-man have been betrayed throughout their life. So take some positives from these. Krishna, Kabir, Jesus, Meera, Mohammed have all been put into betrayal.

A disproportionate shout always hurts others and you also. When there is such an impulse, take a pause and think about how to negate those.

Many times it is obvious that even though there is no harm done by others to us, we perceive their action wrong and injurious. Hence we show impulsive outbursts. Here we need to understand each other to reduce stress and realize our impulsive harmful emotions are our own creations.

If any two members of the same institute, faculty, family, or neighbour are angry with each other they need to express their concern and need for understanding each other and then negotiate for a solution.

The conclusion is every anger, tantrum, or aggressive impulse needs positive attention.

If you have a good, friendly, and positive relationship with others, at your need they will show a positive attitude towards you.

Seeking help or showing a helping attitude:
- Behaviour that is self-injurious and injurious to others should be handled by a middle man to whom the person respects or listens.
- **The person who shows aggressive behaviour does have a severe insecure feeling of getting lost midway. So he has to be counselled that losing a game can open doors for many other events.**
- Using defence mechanism Projection would resolve anger, is however not very true, because your accumulated anger which you could not act out outside like in your office, public places, those are vented out in your house and you get different ways to modify your anger. So in reality your suppressed anger at a later stage is more destructive.
- A person who is angry but rationalizing as not angry is not going to help others or himself. Rather the intensity and the future chance of anger increase.

The most efficient way by which you can be anger free is just to withdraw from the situation.

This should be done just to avoid sudden, impending destruction. But the more you do this, you will create negativity and passive aggression within yourself. So neither your external aggressive behaviour is healthy nor the internal passive aggression is healthy. Both are injurious to self and others, in different magnitudes. The person who suppresses his anger, hostility continuously is very likely to develop many psychological illnesses like sleep disorder, depression, suicide attempts, and may develop a bipolar spectrum illness. They also are at risk of developing physical illnesses like cardiac diseases, stress-induced problems like diabetes mellitus.

Suggestions

- Do not accumulate aggressive impulses internally.

- Speak out your difficulties to others or a third party whom you believe they can help you.
- Realize your own areas of dysfunction which is causing aggression and make a solution.
- Do not act impulsively on your aggressive thoughts.
- At the end of the day forget about your day-long hard time and find a little way of relaxation.
- Think positive.
- Do not make a punishing statement to somebody who has had behaved erratically with you. If so you are making the person's erratic behaviour more (intensely) erratic.
- If you are accumulating aggression in your mind, accept it and realize this will harm you. Find a mentor to help you out of this situation.
- If you are hurt by somebody's behaviour talk to yourself that he/she might have done this by mistake. Tell the Almighty to forgive them for their unconsciously driven anger.
- If you are the one who is doing wrong to others and you realize it, then surrender yourself to the Almighty by accepting your wrongdoings and rectify those.
- Ask an excuse to the person whom you have shown aggression.

If the victim is of the same power as the one who shows aggressive behaviour, then the following may happen:

- Always both parties are very much inquisitive.
- Paranoia present in both.
- Biased behaviour.
- Very poor interpersonal relationships in the family and with friends.
- High hostility range.
- These people make gangs fight with others.

Solutions of Aggressive Behaviour

- Counselling for developing an empathetic attitude and emotional behaviour.
- Knowing what is wrong and what is right in a particular circumstance.
- Giving training to face hostile behaviour from others.
- Giving training to solve Aggressiveness generated because of socioeconomics problems.
- Therapist to give training for desensitization, increasing sustained anger, social skills, religious orientation.
- The person should learn quickly about the ambiguity of the anger evoking situation and act accordingly.
- The counsellor should give insight-oriented counselling to the person who is having aggressive behaviour and make him learn to adjust to different situations and people.
- Counselling may be of different types like – individual, group, brief, long-term therapies. Behaviour therapy also is a model of important therapy in changing behavioural patterns.
- Laws should be addressed for aggression prevention.

How to Work with Aggressive Children and Their Behaviour

1. **To listen to the historical background of the child.**
2. **Analyzing and solving the probable provocating factors of aggression:**

   - Childhood guilt.
   - Poor self-esteem.
   - Poor control over their own impulses.
   - Poor decision making.
   - Prejudices against the close people whom they come across – like parents, siblings, mentors, etc.

- Childhood fear, passiveness, and active anger and its developmental reason.
- Role model if any for the same behavioural pattern.
- Living in a situation of aggressive behaviour for a period till adolescent age – like in family and peer groups.
- Pathological parenting, substance abuse, and abnormal social costumes.
- Pathological brain functioning.
- Minimal brain damage giving rise to mental retardation and ADHD symptoms.

Family Practice and Influence

- Traditional family values, rules, customs should be discussed within the family or in a family get together and involve the child in those discussions.
- There should be a promoter of these values, rules into the problem children.
- Interactive family programmes with formal activities will encourage behaviourally the disturbed children to learn how to modify their inappropriateness of behaviour.
- Too much of family activities, discussions till late at night is deterrent to these type of aggressive behaviour.

Especially for children, their routine timings for study; play, and sleep timing should be maintained.

Developing Some Spiritual Practices Helps a Lot

- Morning prayer.
- Relaxation time, exercising in the morning and doing meditation.
- Baseline morning, afternoon, evening time behaviour should be recorded and accordingly plans of therapy should be planned out.
- Anything difficult to cope up should be kept out for a later discussion.

Reinforcement

For positive growth in a child's behaviour, positive reinforcement by parents, counsellor, or mentor is essential.

Behavioural Practices

- Daily practices to reduce negative impacts of behaviours on education, coping styles should be explained.
- Sudden impulsive behaviours should be controlled by repeated practice by different techniques like:

  - Thought blocking.
  - Relaxation – Deep breathing.
  - Doing some minor acts other than which causes particular impulsive behaviour.
  - Imagery – Walking out from the place to some other place around for a short period.
  - The consequences of impulsive behaviour should be considered for changing the behaviour.

- The counsellor, parents should explain the behaviour of the child, its consequences, and a model change in behaviour to the child.
- All pertaining questions of the child regarding the original behaviour and the changed behaviour should be explained.
- Model behaviour always should be practically shown to the child.
- Giving choices of doing one of two works to get a desirable behaviour, not imposing any behaviour to adopt is a better way of helping the child. As the child who is having aggressive behaviour is emotionally very unstable and his attention, concentration levels are poor so he unlearns things very soon. However, he is tuned for aggressive behaviour. So he quickly learns a more intense aggressive behaviour.
- The counsellor should explain the consequences of the choices.
- Do not allow the child to develop transference.

- Do not allow too many bargains or excuses by the child.
- When the counsellor feels a little encouragement is required to decrease the undesirable behaviour can use it.

During the active phase of the child's aggressive behaviour a counsellor/therapist/parents should do:

- Try to just make him calm without discussing any major issue.
- Try to shift the place of current aggression temporarily.
- To tell the child to cool down behaviourally for now.
- Do not give any positive or negative reinforcement instantly.
- The child should be kept away from others. It lessens the emotional lability.
- Tell the child a few acceptable behavioural patterns.
- Appropriately do some physical restrainment.
  (If there is a risk of self-injurious behaviour, injury to others, chances of absconding, damage to essential elements).
- Do not give contradictory statements.
- As a counsellor when you feel there is a danger of physical harm by the child, keep always a distance.
- Things that need punishment:
- When the child is damaging property, insulting family members and parents, life-threatening behaviour to self and others.
- Bullying behaviour, borderline and antisocial activities, (abnormal conduct) violating social rules which make serious discord.
  (Legal action may be considered now).

Post Aggressive Behaviour Counselling

Deal with the damages the child has done with no regret. Work with resolute.

Give some work to be completed within a time frame to rehabilitate the child.

Give some insight into the future and train him with some work.
Ensure the child to regulate emotions and operate those appropriately.
Make the child learn a few techniques like:

- Thought block, thought elimination.
- Instant relaxations – Immediate changing the place for a little time.
- Think positive about the future.
- Talking to self positively.

Positive reinforcement should be given to the child not before he finishes the task assigned to him for rehabilitation.

Usually, children should be assigned with educational tasks or some skilled one.

* It is important to keep it in mind the post aggressive behaviour. Counselling should always be centred around the positive aspects.

Before reinforcing a positive behaviour just watch and observe for a certain period how the behaviour is going on whether positively or not.

Encouraging and rewarding positive behaviour and observing it for a sustained period can help in removing the bad behaviour.

Counselling and rehabilitation for such children and youth should be for duration till he adopts another positive behaviour and performs well.

A good gesture, moral values, empathetic attitude of the counsellor can make the child learn in a more sensitive and acceptable pattern.

Summary

1. Make realize the children that they are showing a distorted aggressive behaviour. Make them accept it and after a pause to write down the events.
2. Make the children analyze their aggression whether it is justified or not.
3. Accept your erratic behaviour.

4. Do not generate guilt feelings in you rather once for all you forgive
    yourself.
5. Do behaviour modifications.

Couple Therapy

Marital counselling/therapy also called couple/spouse therapy is considered as a sub-branch of family therapy. **Here the focus is predominantly given to couples at risk (troubled couples).**

Techniques broadly used are **behavioural modifications** and **cognitive approaches.**

Methods of counselling may not be different for different groups of couples starting from job variations, geographical variation, family and social structure, education, and financial condition but the approach and explanation/guidance with examples may be different.

The Common Cause of a Marital Conflict

1. Maladjustment
2. Behaviour which is apparently inappropriate to either of the couples.
3. Underlying neuroticism.

The Goal of the Therapy

1. Not only to treat the couple in living but to give a better living to the entire family.
2. Reconstructing the situation.
3. Reconstructing maladaptive behaviour.

History – it goes to the ancient period of Mahabharata and Ramayana in Hindu cultures. It may be traced back to the New Testament. But professionally the knowledge of marital counselling emerged as establishments during the 1920s and afterwards many establishments and many amendments have come up till now.

Ethical Issues

1. To decide who is the patient.
2. To decide what type of therapy (techniques) to be used.
3. To maintain rapport.
4. To know the suggestibility of the client for therapy.
5. To decide the duration of the therapy and when to terminate the therapy.

Principles of Couples Counselling

- Counsellors when interacting with the personal issues of couples they learn to give high-quality therapy and even their own awareness of the problem increases.
- There should be a specific time frame within the initial 1-2 sessions when the counsellor can start a therapeutic alliance and gradually that can be strengthened with the process.
- Counsellors should learn communication skills to alleviate their own stress.
- The primary skill of a counsellor.

  - Open-ended questioning.
  - Showing an emphatic attitude.
  - Silence listening.
  - Eye contact.
  - Gesturing.

Open-ended questioning is to gather more and more information regarding the problem and the client.

Techniques of marital therapy: (Development and maintenance of relationships).

1. Emotion transfer theory – based on **social learning theory** (Albert Bandura). This facilitates to improve the relationship.
2. Social exchange theory – B Thibaut & Kelley.

3. Growth and Decline Relationship – By Levinger and Snock.

4. Object relation theory – based on **psychoanalytic theory**. This improves attachment and empathetic relationships.

    1. In marital counselling many techniques/theories are helpful using the therapy.

    2. Social exchange theory:

       By Thibaut and Kelley, 1959, 1978.
       This theory explains the significance of the interdependence of social relationships. The quality of the outcome depends on the behaviour of both spouses.

    3. Growth and Decline of relationship:
       Change in nature of the relationship as they develop from the point of initial contact between individuals to a level of intimate involvement. This facilitates the attainment of goals.

Growth of relationship (Levinger and Snock 1972)

1. Zero contact ----------------------> O O
   (Two unrelated persons)

2. Awareness ----------------------> O O
   (Unilateral impressions
   but no interaction)

3. Surface contact ------------------------> OO
   (Bilateral attitudes
   and some interaction)

4. Mutuality
   (3.1 Minor intersection) -------------------------> O
   (3.2 Major intersection) -------------------------> ⵝ
   (3.3 Total unity) -------------------------> ●

The above way through the steps a good relationship and total unity can occur. (Applicable for all interpersonal relationships including marital relationship).

(1) **(i) Social learning theory:** (Later social learning theory)

By Bandura A.,

This theory explains many behaviours can be learnt in later childhood. This needs three things: (a) a model, (b) an imitator, (c) an observational behaviour. The observational behaviour and the learning process should be vicarious. The imitator gets a vicarious reinforcement. Most of those who need behavioural correction can be given counselling based on the above theory. Usually, this is very much effective in changing behavioural patterns in psychological entities like phobia, severe depression leading into hopelessness, social withdrawal, stress, aggressive behaviour, pro-social behaviour, sex roles and need for achievement.

During marital counselling this theory can be explained to the couples to modify their sex roles, resolving conflicts, and reducing aggressive behaviour.

(ii) Skinner's Radical Behaviourism: This theory is based on reinforcement and punishment for a particular behaviour to have an observable change in the same. For Skinner B.F. (1953, 1971) personality is a collection of reinforced responses. So it can be changed by conditioning.

When an idea comes to a man to write a poem, the man is not creative. It is the very process of the idea. Similarly, when a woman gives birth to a baby, the woman is not creative. It is the sort of work woman does like a woman.

The above theory is behaviourism. Using this theory, counselling is given for modifying behaviour (Used in changing childhood, adult, and seductive behaviour).

Types of cognitive distortions that affect marital relationships:

1. Beliefs regarding change: "The relationship can never improve."
2. Self-justifying beliefs: "I am right." "The partner is wrong."
3. Reciprocal behaviour: First the partner.
4. Partner is blamed: My partner is the misery of my life.

The above views are kept in marital disputes and these can be attempted to be resolved with **cognitive modification**.

1. Psychodynamic Theory: Here the dynamic issues are discussed like – (a) Nature of relationship of the couple to each other, the relationship of the couples either or both to the third party in the family or society who is concerned. (b) Personal meaning of the relationship. (c) Orientation to the relationship.
2. Insight-oriented therapy: Here the goal is to explore the unconscious probing into the problem till there is acceptance of therapy by the couple.
3. Cognitive therapies: Using this method the therapist tries to change the thought distortions of the client to a realistic and positive change in his or her thoughts.

How to Guide with Positive Thoughts

1. Know the quantum and reality of your verbalization and impulsive behaviour.
2. Realize that it started with a base that may or may not be worth verbalizing.
3. Do not make others responsible for your actions.
4. Do not lay yourself too much down with guilt.
5. Stay conscious and judgemental regarding your own act of impulsivity and aggression.
6. Pinpoint the cause and effect. Try to make a solution to those.
7. If you have any conflicting/aggressive situation with your spouse, accept it.
8. Initially think that your behaviour might have some valid reason and hence do not ignore it. Think over it and you will find it does not have a reason for vengeance.
9. Do not make your conflicts interjected. Find a little time to discuss the problem when you both are a little away from your routine family life.

10. Do not presume anything from your spouse's behaviour regarding the conflict. Make it clean, otherwise, it will be lifelong grief.

11. Try to be calm when the other is arrogant and at the same time try to know about the reason for the same.

12. Many times you might have realized from your past experiences that there comes nothing out of an argument. So stay out of the argument.

13. For an understanding relationship with your spouse explain your problem to your spouse before commenting.

During marital counselling, the prime effort is to make the couple's relationship sustained without a long period of controlling each other's behaviour. However, chances to be given to each other to express their own problem to understand each other. But a long period of constrained relationship would make both the spouse seriously mentally disturbed.

During the process of counselling if no positive results come after a fairly good number of sessions (number of sessions should be around six or the counsellor to decide).

Mostly couples for their problem to solve they should follow the following;

- Tell your problems, goals, and targets to the counsellor.
- Find a way to resolve your emotional difficulties with the help of a counsellor.
- Always look for simultaneous ways of conflict resolution.
- Find out the social support from where you can get some mental support.

Transactional Analysis in Marital Counselling

Transactional analysis of the psychological theory and practical guidelines were given by Eric Berne. Basically, this theory is most applicable for the parent, child counselling, and a qualitative ego analysis. However, it can be used in all human behavioural conflict for resolution.

During my psychiatry practice of more than two decades my most favoured area of work has been counselling, psychotherapy apart from clinical psychiatry.

Here in this chapter, I tried to use a few positive thought applications to the TA method.

Sometimes usually at the conclusive part of counselling therapy (only after few sessions) when the client and the counsellor feel that they are approaching the qualitative end part, the counsellor may use the techniques of TA the 'I am ok' 'You are ok' position.

Few positive steps to consider during the entire process of counselling through T. A.

- The awareness of the conflicting situation.
- The ability to directly interpreting the situation and receiving inputs from the significant others.
- There should be no dilemma considering the ways of action.
- Do a subjective examination of yourself in conflicting situations and you will find a way.

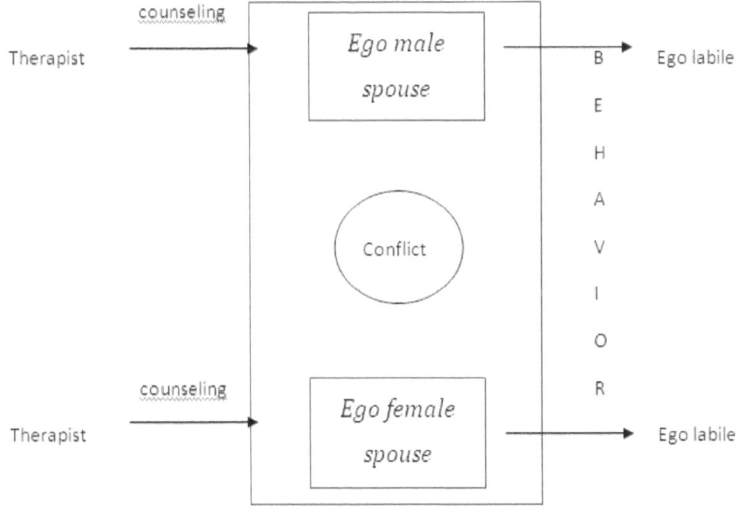

Here only the ego structure is dealt with by the therapist.

Individual sessions are taken for both the spouse.

This is the 1st step of the therapy (Counselling).

In the second stage, the conflict is dealt with.

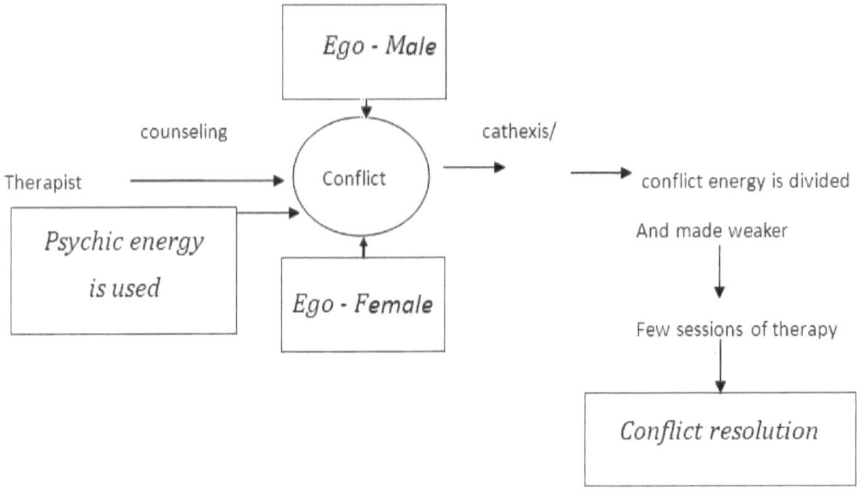

Furthermore, a few points should be considered by the clients as advised by their therapist.

- To increase **motivation** for a change towards positive growth in the relationship.
- **Clients should be aware of what they should change at which stage of therapy.**
- Compliance should be intact.
- Consider certain points that they want to have a re-decision in the next stage of therapy.
- Learn new ideas, techniques from the therapist which can resolve your conflicts.

Illustration: Comparisons, anecdotes, inspiring thoughts can be used by the therapist to strengthen explanations.

(TA Eric Berne).

- Once in a while, 100% of couples have marital distress.

- 10-20 % of couples in India have got strong constraints.
- Most of them (>50%) end up in divorce.
- 20-30 % get separation within 5-10 years.
- 70% get separation within 10-15 years.
- Couple therapy is a clear, evidence-based treatment.
- Couple therapy is basically aimed at:

  a) Resolution of stress.
  b) Prevention of marital discord.

- Couple therapy is given if there is:
- The health problem with the child.
- Poor education of children.
- Faculty support to the family.

Marital stress causes intensely symptomatic disorders in various DSM IV disorders.

For people who have depressive, anxiety, mood disorders, and other psychotic disorders, to them, couple therapy is very effective.

Couple Therapy (The Recent Histories)

Gulman and Fraenkel (2002) described 4 phases:

1. Write down a format for the therapeutic intervention after taking the history.
2. Analyze psychological aspects.
3. Relate it with theoretical processes.
4. Concluding suggestion.

Couple Therapy The Foundation

1. The judgement of the personality structures of the couple who comes for therapy.
2. History taking, diagnosis.
3. A silent decision by the therapist who needs more therapy and who has more problem adjusting.
4. Plan for further presentation of constrained relationship.
5. Treatment of dispute.
6. More distressed couples show – in suggestibility, contempt, criticizing the other.
7. As the cognitive functions of distressed couples are distorted counsellors/therapists need to deal with those negative cognitions and giving support and repeated counselling for resolution of the fact they face.
8. Initially, both the couples may come for therapy, but in between, one may withdraw. In this case, the other spouse should talk to the partner or with the help of a third party may be brought again for counselling. And now the couples should be given a strong message for a positive future.
9. The couple's personality, emotion, and behaviour should be taken into account for planning and continuing the therapy.
10. Couples should be given the same invention for completing it from which assessment would be better.

Therapy

Aim at modifying the behaviour:

- Each time the couple shows any negative behaviour that multiplies negative feelings and behaviour in the partner and also adds on to the anger/aggression on to self.
- Positive behaviour would make the other couple/spouse influenced and increase his/her behaviour in a positive manner.

- Apply and consider tips that can increase positive behaviour, like going together for some social function, dinner, movies, etc.
- The therapist/counsellor should aim at; a) modifying the undesired behaviour and b) increasing communication with one another.
- While giving therapy to one partner the therapist should carefully listen to the other partner and give an acceptance smile.

Aim at modifying the distorted cognition:

- In a state of conflicts between couples the basic reason mostly is a distorted perception of the relationship, communication, and behaviour. So once the distorted cognitions are modified through CBT there appears an increased quality of understanding.
- Couple conflicts primarily arise when one of the partner's basic needs like – appreciation, affiliation, love, intimacy, and sex are not met with.
- So during behaviour modification always it should be explained regarding the needs and appropriateness of the above.
- Couple conflicts secondarily arise when one partner with an unmannered way describes, accepts, or ignores the primary causes of the conflicts, like – aggressive behaviour, avoiding to listen or see to the partner, and physical assault.

Structuring the Therapy

- Define the factors which cause stress between the couples.
- Give axis-I, II, III diagnosis for both couples if possible.
- Find out who should be given more importance for counselling considering the severity of symptoms/stress.
- Define the goals of counselling.

- Define the targets of counselling in the initial 2-3 sessions considering both the individuals' views.
- As couple therapy is a very sensitive issue the number of therapy sessions would be more than counselling for other ailments.
- (in my clinical practice I prefer to extend therapy sessions up to 6-15 sessions.)
- Selected use of words, phrases, and stepwise questioning should be done.
- Situations, events which give a negative impact on the couple should be solved in a guided and selective way.
- Home works should be given.
- Reorientation, reevaluation of thoughts, and beliefs of the couple should be encouraged.

* * *

- Future effects of the relationships should be considered by the couple considering the positive and negative sides.
- The emotional aspects of the couple should be considered by the therapist to improve positive progress.
- Acceptance of each other's behaviour reduces earlier conflicts.
- If any behaviour seems irreparable, just try to find out the source of the same behaviour and try to resolve the conflict at the same.
- Each conflict should be aimed at different times and in different ways.
- During the course of acceptance of some behaviours of the partner, he or she may feel demoralized but the issue can be solved if he or she remains at ease.

Emotional Focus of Couple Therapy

- Understanding of each couple's emotional state, emotional factors, and emotional ailments.

- Improving the emotional bonds between couples in different ways like – recreational activities, policymaking, – compliance with each other's emotional feelings, and – restructuring the emotional expressions.
- Introduce a mutual alliance.
- Introduce simple, rational ways of dealing with the couple's emotional state.
- Give value to the couple's social, cultural, academic, and economic status.
- Usually, emotional problems start from past or present relationship problems. So the problem of intimacy starts. Hence past relationships and their problem should be dealt with effective action by counselling.
- Improve relationship skills.
- Analyze the source of stress and make the couple learn how to nullify their relationship stress.

Short Term Couple Therapy:

- The basic aim of the therapy should be given to the current areas of conflict.
- Deal the conflicts between the couples and also deal with the individualized stress which makes the spouse excentric.
- Improve relationship-improving skills.
- Take the risk to handle the discord.
- Improve rational ways of thinking.
- Sessions should be given to family members and significant others separately.

Skills of Counsellor Undertaking Couples Counselling

1. **Insight of counsellor's own beliefs:**

    - The counsellor should know that his beliefs regarding the client's problem and the situation will affect counselling in a variety of ways. The counsellor should not directly use his own bias, emotions of his problem for establishing a therapeutic relationship, rather he must use his self-awareness, should understand the intensity of the client's problem and proceed to alleviate the symptoms.

    - The insight of the counsellor would provide a better quality of counselling.

    - All counsellors should regularly review their personal issues and beliefs to improve their counselling skills and to know when and how to make a full stop in interfering with counselling sessions.

    - Insight of the counsellor into his beliefs allows him to be non-partial to the client's situation.

2. **Counsellor's Tolerability:**

    - Couples counselling is very much emotionally oriented. So the counsellor should analyze critically, and maintain a sustained alliance with the couple, and hope for fair improvement.

    - The counsellor should encourage the couple to express their problem honestly and faithfully.

    - Once the reliability between the counsellor and the couple is established the entire process of counselling will improve the problem of the couple.

3. The counsellor should have complete knowledge (scientific) over the couple's issue so that he can validate it and give strong suggestions to the couples.

4. **Understanding the couple's behaviour:**

    ▪ The counsellor should understand the couple's problem and should know when and what to probe. The counsellor also should protect the couple's desire regarding their relationship.

    ▪ All the socio-cultural, economic, and educational status should be respectfully considered. An individual should be given equal preference as others.

    ▪ The counsellor should give support to the couple and give positive empowerment.

5. The counsellor may transfer his/her emotions of relationships with his/her partner or other family members to the couple resulting in the poor therapeutic alliance and poor improvement.

    ▪ The counsellor should be having no bias for both couples.

    ▪ Whatever the current relationship the couples have, you (counsellor) should respect those and respect the couple's wish. This will facilitate the interaction of couples with the counsellor.

    ▪ Allow dialogues between the couples and those will clear their misunderstanding in many instances.

    ▪ The counsellor should take an active role in understanding difficult issues with the couples and try to resolve those and try to reduce the undesired behaviour of the couple.

    All the above facilitate a desirable couple's behaviour and build a sustainable, reliable relationship with both partners.

6. **Making A Therapeutic Alliance:**
    The alliance means a relationship between the counsellor and the couple in a working situation. It should be an agreed-upon relationship. The process of an alliance gives access to:

- Remaining involved in the session,
- Find out the events on which the work should be done.

To maintain a persistent alliance the counsellor should follow the steps like:

1. **Acceptance and Acknowledgement.**

    - Here the counsellor should accept and acknowledge the view of the couple.
    - During the process of counselling, the couple should be given appropriate regard, response, and reciprocal communication (show soothing gestures).
    - The counsellor should speak to both the partners at different times.
    - The counsellor should evaluate and validate the couple's problem and their respectfulness to each other.
    - The counsellor should assist the couple to know and value their respective values, ideas, past history, and future expectations.
    - The counsellor should constantly guide to resolve the discord of both partners.

2. The second most important aspect of making an alliance with a couple is the knowledge of the counsellor regarding the couple's counselling and competence.
3. The counsellor should be considerate, punctual, and emphatic to the couple and the process of counselling.

Model of Counselling with the Couple

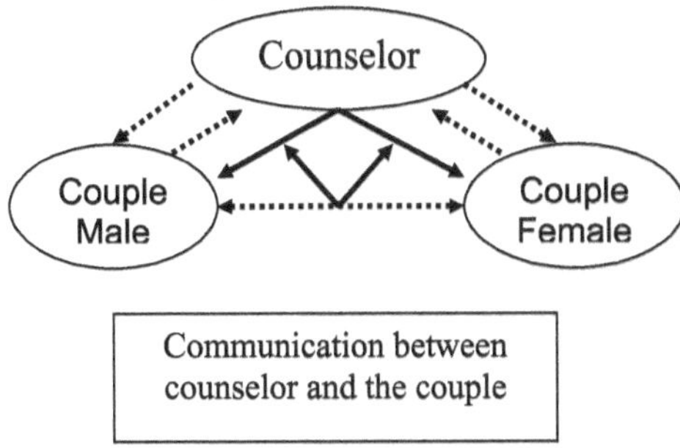

Direct communication forms a relationship which is reliable and result oriented by the counsellor with the couple.

Here introductory questioning can be done with the couple.

Communication between both partners:
This process will allow a better relationship between the partners, a better understanding of each other's problems, better solutions to problems, and a better bond between the couples. The counsellor here acts as a moderator.

- Role model.
- Mediator.
- Opportunity provider for effective communication with the clients (couple).

Effective behaviour mediator:

- To remain subdued when the other partner is communicating.
- Just be concerned with your present.
- Few possible plans may be made for the future.
- Do not probe into hostile feelings.
- The couple should be reminded about their role in the therapy.

Marriage and Family Counselling

- General thoughts, ideas, and acts do not always reflect the relationship problem. The response of both partners which are continually expressed and reflected outwardly and that affects in a sustainable way the other partner are the real problem in a relationship.
- Always the core dynamics of the relationship are in a process of change.

Interventions: To intervene with the core issues that are changing the dynamics. Example of changing dynamics – Earlier weekend holidays being stopped. Intervention in the relationship may start with weekend holidays may take a course of family get together.

Families those are in stress and suffering from its bad effect are not pathological rather they are not just finding a way to cope with the stress.

Families those need counselling usually have:

1. **Stress because of anticipated events like:**

   - Adolescent crisis, education, failure, marriage, job, leaving at a parental place, childbirth, gender-specific role, either not followed or overburdened.
   - Death, children leaving home.
   - Serious physical and mental illness.

2. **Stress because of unexpected events like:**

   - Financial loss, natural calamities.

- Job stress and loss/change in job.
- Family and social violence.

Family members who face stress, they usually get disconnected from others (family as well as societal members).

They develop anxiety. The therapist's role is to generate confidence in those members to start a relationship with another member who can have intimacy with him/her.

Often a distressed family member does have:

- Poor responsibility
- Poor tolerance
- Poor and distorted cognitions
- Increase the anticipation of threats
- Increase the risk of showing a rebellious attitude against his parents or other members of his family.
- Increase the risk of showing social and antisocial behaviour.

Often a distressed family to reconcile with the situation may:

- Make certain changes in their family norms to have better adaptability.
- Change some pre-existing norms

Here the therapist helps the family members with the above reassertions. Also, build a positive attitude towards **family values** and **cultural affirmations.**

Also, educational, socio-economic conditions should be taken care of.

Process of the Counselling

- Making a decision to suggest a particular couple for counselling and taking consent from the couple for counselling.

- Giving introduction sessions of counselling to all the family members.
- Trying to make an informative, faithful, and collaborative relationship with the couples in stress.
- Assessing the family's socio-cultural, education, language values, and norms are essential.
- The counselling process should always continuously aim at the transactional/interactional points. These are the target points by probing which the clients/couples come out with their stressful and conflicting situations.
- The counsellor then tries to resolve the conflict and make the client reasonably relaxed. Now the clients become more confident about the process of counselling.
- Each client is then made aware of his/her part in the family responsibilities and particular assignments are given to them which should be followed up, regulated by the counsellor.
- There should be a progressive active and direct communication between the member of the couple and the counsellor. This helps in generating more psychic strength in the couple.
- **One of the most important aspects of the process of marital counselling is redefining the relationship between the couple.**

The counsellor should focus on:

- How to resolve the conflict not too much on the content of the conflict.
- The dynamics of family relationships not too much on thoughts, images, and emotions.
- More on current stressful issues first then switch over to past issues/contents.
- Direct communication with an individual spouse.
- Positive reinforcement for working intensely with the spouse.
- The commonalities between both spouses.
- Resolving issues with their own family and in-laws.

Certain things the counsellor should ask the couple individually:

- How is your relationship with your parents and in-laws?
- How is the relationship between the parents and in-laws with you?
- How is your relationship with your other family members and in-law's family members?
- Can you establish a soothing relationship with your family members and with in-law's family members?

Typical Problems of the Couples

- One of the couple too much busy in his/her job, the rest of the members of the family especially the children suffer.
- Marital disputes start because of the child's mental health and future planning. This usually leads to a constrained sexual life between both partners.
- Many times in recent years both male and female they have forgotten their gender role specification, especially females when going out for job leaving their children quite alone at the home or other places. Studies have found that these children have become more antisocial, borderline, drug addicts, etc. So each point should be discussed with the counsellor at a time and find a solution.
- One of the most suitable and acceptable ways of dealing with the children who show some rebellious attitude towards the parents that the counsellor, the parents should encourage direct communication with the child, and no apparent confrontation should be there during the process of counselling.
- The rivalry between spouses regarding education, job, financial earnings, social and personal achievements, family, and social

background also becomes a serious stressor and should be holistically resolved.

- Infidelity between the spouses is one of the most difficult areas for counselling and should be dealt with supportive care. Infidelity usually occurs due to a lack of marital intimacy, family burdens, poor communication, addiction-related illness, paranoid personality disorder, and many other issues. Different issues should be dealt with separately, if possible with different techniques and examples (alternative types of counselling).
- The therapist should make clear that to some extent both are responsible and both have to take part to resolve the conflicts.
- The therapist should tell the spouses to tell their need, urge, and suppressed ideas and anger.

Marriage Management

- Know the sanctity, eternity, and core issues of marriage.
- Marriage is a new journey in life for which you have to find out the new coping mechanism, new strength.
- Know what is right and wrong for your marriage and marital life. Ignore those suggestions which you may not feel good for you.
- Take every step cautiously in the initial stages of marriage.
- Marriage is a dynamic and multidimensional change in life.
- It creates personal, interpersonal, developmental, and intergenerational changes.
- Marriage is all about "Trust".

The journey of marriage goes through many different stages. But a prominent survey depicts the following as most important:

1. Compassion for each other.
2. Comfort with each other.
3. Introspection with reality.
4. Conflict and confrontation.
5. Cooping and cooperation.
6. Contemplation.
7. Consonance.
8. Co-creating love.

How to resolve the above issues and get over:

1. Compassion for each other:
   Marriage implies to Love.

   - Save it.
   - Sense it.
   - Speak it.
   - Serve it.
   - Sex intimacy.

2. Comfort with each other:

   - Find your comfort zone and along with your partner's and share it with each other.

3. Introspection with reality:

   - Know your needs and desires from your partner.
   - Have an open discussion where there is a need.
   - Have a sustainable friendly attitude.
   - Have the patience to listen to your partner.
   - Have proper gender-specific family roles.
   - Have appropriate money matters.

4. Conflict and confrontation:
(It starts from the genesis of mine and mine in mind)

- Try to resolve conflicts by shifting conflicts to the act of problem-solving.
- Design individual functions and goals.
- Doubts should be changed to transference.
- Accept both are right and wrong at the same time.

5. Coping with the following:

- Job, Business (work).
- Loss (Financial, Life).
- Disputes in family Friends, Societies.
- Time, Trends, Place.
- Present, Past, Future.
- Sexual relationship.

  - Do your job up to your ability and not compare with others' work.
  - Loss is a process in life. So accept it. Make new financial budgets and new associations.
  - Connect with more friends and family members that would alleviate your level of stress and improve your quality of life.
  - Analyze your past. Make a righteous attitude and have a little dream for the future.
  - Start new ways of lovemaking.
  - Find ways of making your marital life strong.

- Recapitulate your intimate days of marriage.
- Realize that parenthood would make your marriage strong.
- Care for the elderly in the family.

- Support your spouse to reduce his/her stress. Think about your and your spouse's good physical and mental health.

Contemplation:

- See your marriage growing.
- See the new perspectives, the meaning of marriage, and look for the repair of any damage in the relationship.

To Deal with Marriage

Management of marriage which leads to either a successful or default in marriage depends on how the conflict is resolved not just looking into Whether and What conflicts are there in the marital relationship.

To Avoid Significant Negative Attitudes

1. Finding out each and everything that just makes only a difference in opinion.
   Example – This New TV is good, that is bad.
2. Noncompliance –
   Example – Come from the office a little early to go for dinner, coming late.
3. Poor Listening to each other.
   Example – Not heard that you asked for a cup of coffee.
4. Criticizing each other (the couples) is damaging to the relationship. It is more serious than making some arguments. The statements like "You can never be changed" are seriously damaging.

Infidelity is more serious than just making a joke.

5. **Contempt:**
   This is truly torturous in the life of a spouse. This brings serious issues like marital violence, disrespect to each other. This process of contempt if is repeated demoralizes partners

and they may fall into severe reactive depression, drug abuse and also may go for antisocial and self-injurious behaviour.

Most often neurotic and immature defence mechanisms may play the role of the leader and these are not healthy for family relationships.

Hostility usually starts at a later stage of contempt and unresolved conflict. The process of reconciliation is blocked in this stage.

Feelings of high self-esteem also one of the main factors in the process of contempt.

Cautious resolution with a passion for these factors needed for healthy family life.

6. **Negative attitude and behaviour which aggravates marital disputes:**

- Blaming the aggressive behaviour of the partner in front of others.
- Negative propaganda of the partner regarding character, attributions, addictions.
- Hostile withdrawal from interaction.
- Over bordering with emotional projections from the partner often make the other partner just a passive listener. Sometimes the more vocal partner makes the other a passive listener and makes him/her responsible for everything.

If all the above categories of interactions are present then the relationship would look futile and ends up in early almost first five years of marriage. But couples who are having the above conflicts but are not too much concern for each other their relationship usually dies after 10 years or so.

Ways to make positive growth in marital disputes

- **Aggressive, conflicting, and emotional flooding:**

  - Quit the discussion for the time being. Give yourself rest. Release your anxiety by taking deep breaths and a little walking. Engage in other activities.

- **Encapsulate situations:**

  - Few conflicting matters never get solved and if tried, those generate new problems. So for such problems, think over it, realize the outcome and make your mind peaceful to the extent you can. Leave everything on time.

- **Trying to win over the other:**

  - Just try to make a mutual agreement. This will reduce dispute escalations.

- **Early intervention:**

  - Conflict understanding
  - Realization of conflict keeping one's own perspective.
  - Try to take help from others to have some positive advice.
  - Reduce your anxiety by appropriate means.
  - Use your defence mechanisms.
  - Resolve your conflicts.

- **Use of humour**
- **Mutual positive reinforcements**
- **Never go through your diary of looking into the past where emotionally torturing events are mentioned.**

✷ ✷ ✷

The counsellor should aim at:

- Starting the old relationship with new perspectives.
- Making understand the couples what marriage means. 1) Their own view 2) holistic view.
- Making the couples understand that relationship always takes a different meaning familiarly, personally, financially, and socially.
- Allowing the couples to know the past trends of marriage and take some positive from it.
- Discussing the positive ways couples live when their marriage is a happy one. During periods of some conflict, they should discuss their early happy days and talk about the positives and not being too crude for negative points.
- Happy couples more frequently save their major life events even though those are a bit worrisome for the spouse.
- Happy couples highlight their struggle in their communication and these make the relationship more strong.
- If the couples live unhappily the counsellor should aim to deal with the

  - Aggression and negative feelings towards the spouse.
  - Discrimination between the spouses.
  - Sense of dishonour and worthless feelings.
  - Use of 'I' and 'me' to change it to the feelings of "we-ness" Example – We purchased the car.

Parenthood makes most of the marriage soothing and stable although many transitions may have happened. The husband's acceptance to become a father and the wife's readiness to bear the pain of childbirth resolves many misunderstandings.

Stress and Counselling

Human beings are interlinked with the effects of stress psycho physiologically despite the many discoveries in modern science about stress. But certainly, there is a cutoff point that exists between body and mind. So definitely we can deal with stress, either we cope or not.

Stress is an integral part of human life. Everything which we see like survival, violence, disease, death all involve stress.

"Stress is how badly we react with the situation."

All diseases involve stress but many diseases are directly related to stress like cardiovascular illnesses, gastrointestinal disorders, skin diseases, and almost all chronic illnesses. Sometimes stress positively modifies human behaviour as explained by Berthold "Anxiety is the mother of motivation."

Levitt also described stress/anxiety that can impel us for self-improvement, self-analysis, behavioural modification, achievement, and success.

Recently it has been scientifically proved that amongst all illnesses stress and other psychological illnesses are the reason for a high percentage and hence a lot of anti-anxiety, hypnotics, and sedatives are used in daily practice by the doctors and as well self-medication. Every day more than a million dollars is spent on just sedatives and hypnotic abuse.

At the end of the day, you compare a hard working day and a day during which you just listen to some aesthetic/spiritual talks/music you will find after a hard working day you hardly are getting sleep at night whereas during the other some may sleep during the day's programme. This reflects our job is not worth our life. Because sleep is the biggest attribute life has got.

Statistics show around 20 million prescriptions of sedatives are prescribed in America every year and India is also growing up to this severity and will reach soon. More than 1 lac people commit suicide every year in America which significantly shows how stress decimates our lives.

How to React to Stress

1. Know that it was there even before you experienced it.
2. Think about your past when you were cheerful when it (stress) was there.
3. In your unconscious mind if you were dealing with stress you can always deal in your conscious mind.
4. Think that by now you have already started reacting positively to stress.
5. Continue your positivity as per the earlier suggestions.

Correct Your Frequent Problems

1. If you are getting good sleep, it's fine. Otherwise do not think about sleeplessness. Be relaxed and find small ways to resolve this.
2. Before sleep:

    - Try to pass urine and empty your bladder.
    - Wash your feet hands and face.
    - Take a little water or a cup of milk.
    - Avoid talking about addictive substances like – alcohol, sedatives, and smoking, etc.

3. May listen to music (classical).
4. Do not take a heavy dinner.
5. A little exercise in the morning may help you.
6. Do not do extra work during the day.
7. Avoid quarrels and arguments before going to sleep.
8. Do not be a victim of guilt. If it generates within you, accept it generously, and resolve it. Think not to be there in the same

mental state next time. Guilt is the highest self-punishment one gets which usually happens when there is an evil or sad feeling from your mind. You can win devils not stress if you don't understand those.

9. Day's residue: Either the summary of events of the whole day or few major events of the day when perceived during the early or late night sleep is called day's residues. Usually, this is very much disturbing when the person tries to recollect the dream. So forget and forgive all the bad happenings of the day and you will feel relaxed.

10. If anything wrong you did, first you forgive yourself and try not to commit the same again. Be relaxed.

11. Know yourself and know about your problem. Try to get rid of it by your self-knowledge which is the spiritual aspect.

12. If you have some family problems you can share those with your dear friends and try to resolve it.

Stress Inducing Factors

A. Familial and personality factors.
B. Traumatic life events.
C. Faulty childhood development.
D. Faulty psychosocial learning.
E. Other factors that influence daily living.

Few things to know for managing stress:

1. Try to realize what are the stresses inducing situations and what happens when those occur.

2. Think or know about your own present situation.

3. Know how to control your body's reaction to stress those are scary.

4. Understand your stress and think about the measures which can help you.

5. What may be a stress for you may be a joy for others. So it is purely subjective.

What happens when stress occurs:

1. Excessive sensitivity (arousal) for external situations. Cognitive and behavioural disturbances occur when stress occurs.

    Stress either may be caused by an external stimulus or an internal thought – conscious/subconscious and must be fear/anxiety-provoking.

    Once fear is generated in the mind it gradually affects the system of bodily functions.

2. The response of bodily functions to stress creates biochemical changes in the body which can precipitate some external bodily symptoms like – Tremors, Palpitation, Sweating, Increase urination, Increase Blood pressure, Increase Respiration rate, etc.

3. These bodily reactions and symptoms may cope with the stress if it becomes chronic and if the coping mechanism is good.

4. Life events also affect the physical state and emotional aspect of a human being and create stress.

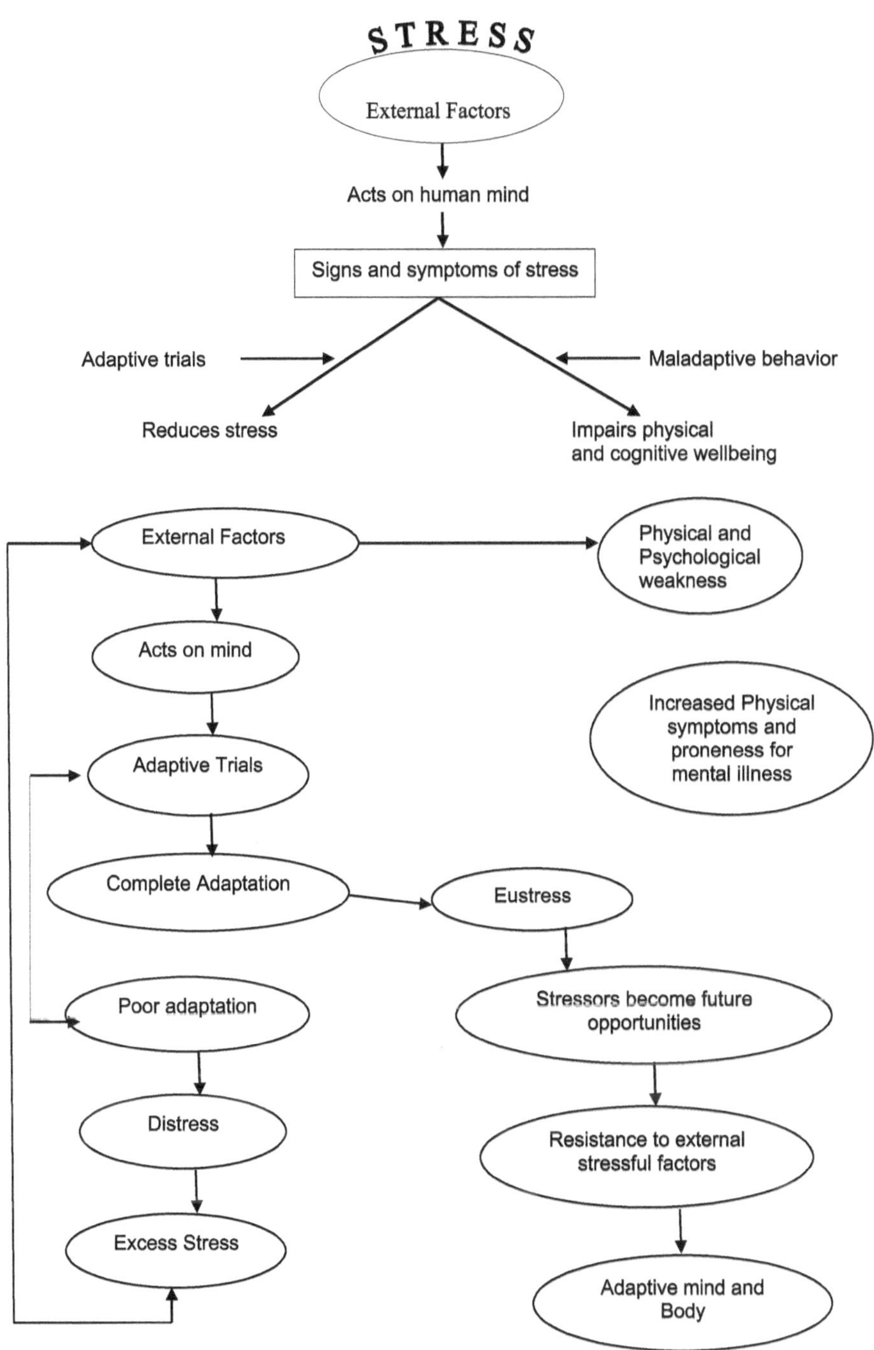
STRESS
External Factors
Acts on human mind
Signs and symptoms of stress
Adaptive trials
Maladaptive behavior
Reduces stress
Impairs physical
and cognitive wellbeing
External Factors
Physical and
Psychological
weakness
Acts on mind
Increased Physical
symptoms and
proneness for
mental illness
Adaptive Trials
Complete Adaptation
Eustress
Poor adaptation
Stressors become future
opportunities
Distress
Resistance to external
stressful factors
Excess Stress
Adaptive mind and
Body

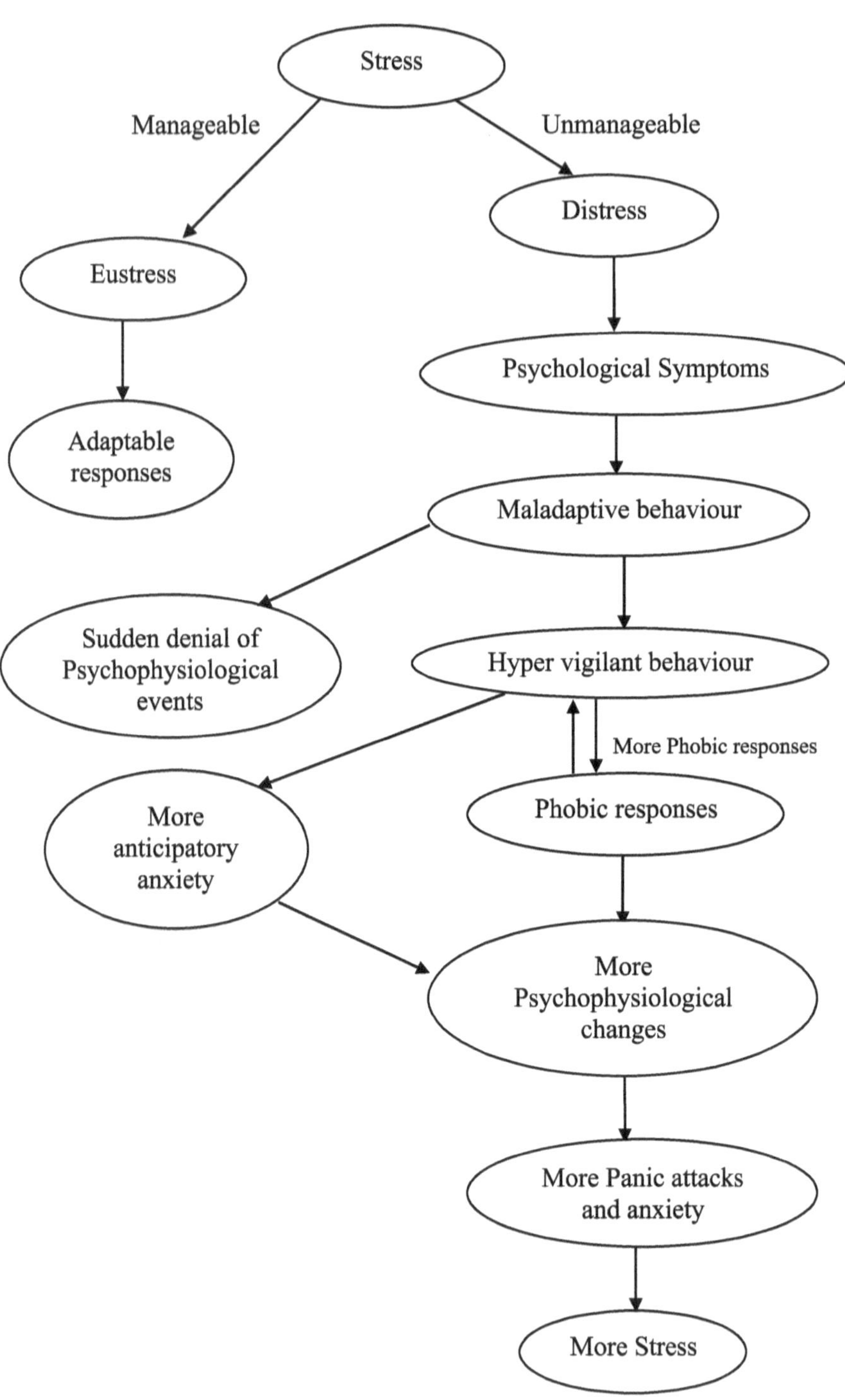
Stress
Manageable
Unmanageable
Eustress
Distress
Psychological Symptoms
Adaptable
responses
Maladaptive behaviour
Sudden denial of
Psychophysiological
events
Hyper vigilant behaviour
More Phobic responses
More
anticipatory
anxiety
Phobic responses
More
Psychophysiological
changes
More Panic attacks
and anxiety
More Stress

Know About Your Stress

1. If you ignore stress every time without thinking about it, a time will come it may look like a huge hood and your restlessness for sure will increase. So do not ignore your stress.
    Try to know the following regarding stress:

    i. Its reason.
    ii. How it affects mental and physical aspects.
    iii.   Its severity.
    iv. How to resolve it.

2. You may write down about your stress and plan how you can manage it.
3. Do not put lots of psychological efforts just to know regarding the causes and course of stress.
4. Ask questions to yourself about the stress and try to get answers from your own logic.
5. Always share your anxiety, worries with someone whom you trust the most.
6. Experience the stress that is happening to you in a very alert state of mind.
7. Once you experience stress, write down a few significant points like:

    a. Reason for the stress.
    b. Major effects of it.
    c. Major precipitating or catalyzing factors.
    d. The way how you can reduce the effects of it.

8. Do not think about the past bad effects of stress nor get apprehension anticipating stress in the future.
9. Make some meaningful strategies for stress those you face.

New ways to find the road to success

1. If you are getting a particular type of stress and you are dealing with it in a particular way for a long time, try to change the way of your attempts to deal with stress, so that you can learn new ways to deal with stress.

2. Do not experiment in dealing with stress by using new ways when it is severe. Because your techniques by then may be faulty.

3. Once you become successful in reducing stress, encourage yourself especially with some recreation.

4. A good bath before dinner may make your sleep better and reduce your stress. The next morning will then be fresh and full of energy.

5. Before you go to sleep empty your mind from all the events of the day.

6. Think that many problems have already come to my life and I have successfully overcome those. So I can win many more.

Avoidance and Anticipatory Anxiety

1. Any stress-inducing event if it had earlier happened to you a few times it might generate an avoidance behaviour to skip from the event.

   - Do not avoid the event. Try to face it and feel the event gleefully.
   - Face imaginary stress and feel the unreality of it and think that all stresses mostly come from external sources and their existence is temporary.

2. Stress inducing thoughts or events create future anxiety even if it is not a current event.

   - Never think about the future. It does not have anything to do with your present.
   - Never think too much repeatedly about a nonexisting event.

3. Anticipating a fear and avoiding the situation makes you lose many cheerful moments of life. So do not panic, do not anticipate fear, and do not have an avoidant behaviour.

4. Worrying about the past events which had some serious impact on your life would always increase stress and its sequel. You should see what you are losing now. So just be conscious of your present.

Stress Resolution

Basic areas to work on:

1. Educate yourself about stress.
2. Develop coping mechanisms for reducing stress.
3. Learn relaxation, meditation, and other procedures to reduce stress.
4. To create an adequate family and social support to reduce stress.

Either you interact/face/counteract with stress till you resolve it or you ignore the stressful event and take a different way. Do not pile up too much stress in your mind for your future.

Here we should always remember that ignoring stress does not mean to accumulate it. If you do it now things may become huge for you sometimes or other and you will be more troubled.

Always it is better to deal with the problem from the first appearance and by doing this you will get your confidence built up and you can manage stressful events in the future.

Your plans and how you should deal with Stress

1. The number and categorize your plans.
2. Divide and group the works/exercises/jobs that are in your plan.
3. Give a certain time to each work. Don't be very strict about your timetable. Be flexible in your work.
4. Don't make your schedule for stress resolution with tough options.

5. Make a very calm and soothing environment at your house/ workplace. Keep your mind calm and cool even your efforts may fail some times.

6. Before starting your work, complete your prior appointments. Make your mind relax with some free time.

7. If you feel very stressed, give a break from your work; Go for a walk and do a little bit of relaxation.

8. If you have disturbance in sleep and you feel stressed, you may do DMR (Deep Muscle Relaxation – Jacobson's), sabasana, etc. (the Yogic exercises).

Make your plans easy

1. Do your work in sessions as per your own convenience initially.

2. Give a little break to your work intermittently.

3. Work regularly.

4. Don't keep too much pending works. You may do gradual work but do it regularly.

    i.   Hence you can reduce your work pressure.
    ii.   You can do better qualitatively and quantitatively.
    iii. You will have low mental and physical exertion.

5. At the end of a work session, just try to ruminate it and get some pleasurable moments out of it.

Music and Relaxation

1. Think of life as DANCE and life events are a little MUSIC of it.

2. Musical waves touch psychic waves very easily and the attribution of the human mind is the most for music.

3. So whenever you are in stress just hear music and be sure you will be there at a relaxing moment.

4. Try to remember the most pleasing tunes/words/lyrics which you can keep in your mind for a long and retrieve it when there is stress.

Make it half or less at a time

1. Think and judge the nature and severity of the stress.
2. To deal with it, make it in parts. Then deal with every part of the event/thought gradually.
3. By doing this the whole stress will seem significantly less.
4. In parts, you can always solve your problems effectively and better.

Counselling in stress-related problems

- When stress predominantly contains emotional content the client seeks counselling to improve psychological well-being.
- This process should generate:-

  1. Comfortable feelings with self and the place, atmosphere, and associated things that relate to the process of counselling.
  2. Good rapport with the counsellor.
  3. Positive reinforcing thoughts in the client's mind.
  4. Positive thinking regarding others.

- Counselling involves personal, job, family, and other significant issues.
- Overwhelming emotional problems which are harmful to their best of interest to be handled immediately keeping in view with their jobs, family, and other aspects of social life.

Counselling increases self-confidence and increases insight into the ability to work effectively

Things done in counselling:

1. Suggestions given: This requires the judgement of the client's problem and to make a structured format of course of action.

Example: Client is having Addiction

- Underlying reason Marital conflict.
- The counsellor should plan for marital therapy, and as well as counselling for increasing motivation for deaddiction.

2. Reassurance: This gives the client who is in a stressful situation, confidence, and courage to face the problem. The client hence generates a feeling of a suitable course of action.

3. Communication: By counselling, the level of communication improves regarding stress. Communication can also help to understand other activities, especially at an organizational level.

4. Catharsis: Counselling in a stressful situation can help clients to release their emotional content. This is called emotional catharsis. Clients during their stressful conditions become dependent on others easily. So in a counselling session, they get an opportunity to tell their views difficulties to the counsellor. During subsequent visits, clients behave in a more relaxed way, talk more relevantly, and also their statements become more rational.

5. Encouragement: The client during the process of counselling is made aware of the responsibilities for handling his/her emotional problems and explained what are the responsibilities and what should be the realistic ways of solving those problems. Example:

- Stressful factor – Examination
- Emotional problem – Sadness/depression
- Responsibility – To appear in the examination
- Realistic way – To think positively and to think he/she can achieve a positive result.

6. Realistic meaning: The counsellor makes the counselee to think more than what he/she has already done for emotional

catharsis. He/she has to be holistically made realize to go through the ego functions to improve the basic goals.

Example: Depression caused by a broken love affair explained to the counsellor. Now the counsellor makes the counselee realized that the first thing is to appear in the examination. And the basic goal to improve skills to get ready for examination with a hope of a good result.

Types of Counselling

1. **Directive counselling**: Here the counsellor talks to the counselee individually and if there is a need of involving a third party who can play a significant role may be involved. Directive counselling deals with reassurance, emotional catharsis, and restructuring distorted thoughts.

2. **Non-directive counselling**: It is a client-centred therapy. It involves skilful listening by both the counsellor and the counselee. There should be indirect encouragement to the client. The counsellor should first understand the troublesome problems and decides on appropriate solutions. The most important advantage of non-directive counselling is to reorient the counselee for attaining the earlier functioning with his/her colleagues, family, and friends.

Reorientation should also be aimed at socio-economic issues.

The model of counselling for stress management also explains regarding – (1) Relaxation, (2) Biofeedback, (3) Meditation, (4) Rehabilitation.

In a stressful situation: If there is a confrontation of any sort it should be dealt with quietly. The client may close his/her eyes for quieting the mental state for some time.

- Take comfortable breathing. May listen to music.
- Create some mental image which can be relaxing.
- Avoid distracting thoughts.

Professionalism in Counselling

1. To make social and organizational equality.
2. The counsellor should listen in a supporting and clear mind to the client.
3. The counsellor should help the client to get an improved way of action with the best of efforts.
4. Counsellor and counselee relationship should be established to exchange the views between them to solve the counselee's problem.
5. The counsellor should keep patience and be supportive of the client.

Managing Examination Stress

Regarding the Preparation

- **Prepare your best that you can.**

    - Do not compare your best to the other's best.
    - Try to understand your own abilities, capabilities.

- **Know how much stress you can handle.**
- **Always try to know from your immediate seniors how they handled the stress of examinations.**

    - You can learn from them the tips regarding the subjects.
    - Only accepts those tips which you can use to get some benefit.
    - Know that your final output for the best result is a sum of your total efforts for the entire year.

- **Basic Steps:**

    - Take an easy subject first.
    - Gradually move into other subjects according to your comfort.
    - Daily give a few hours to each subject, so that it becomes quite familiar to you at the time of examination.
    - Make a time table for the entire week and paste it on the wall of your room.
    - Paste important points, charts, pictures, graphs of the subject on the wall of your room.
    - Do regular revision of the subject as and when required.
    - Identify your problem areas in study and revise it regularly with the help of a senior, class/subject teacher, or a tutor.

- Life events like: Change of hostels/place of stay, marriage, financial stress, planning to have a child doing some new things during or around the examination are stressful. So avoid these things just before an examination.

- **Be careful and do not be in haste:**

  - Do a sequential arrangement for your studies.
  - Time table should be prepared which should have little time for relaxation.
  - Do not be perturbed by your first reading doubts as well as revisions. If you do so it will add to your stress.
  - Every day look at your timetable and follow as much as you can and try to be more competent gradually without taking too much into mind.

- **Study place:**

  - Make your study room comfortable as your own needs like: Open the windows; light up and clean the room, have a slight room perfume spray if you like.
  - Arrange your study materials properly.
  - Try to make the room noise-free.

- **Study period:**

  - During the study when you feel that you are tired enough or cannot give proper attention to your study take a little break for a few minutes.
  - You may go out for a 5-10 minutes break. Take fresh breathing, look around, and be in the sunlight and fresh air. Then do the usual study again.
  - Home study sessions should be 30 minutes and then take a gap for 5-10 minutes.

- Early in the morning start revising your one day ago study quickly.
- Take small intervals in between revision. Do some methodical relaxation. Change your place of study in the same vicinity for a few minutes. All these will reduce anxiety and increase your wish to read.
- During the last few hours of appearing in examination do not change any of the modalities of your revision.

Revising Tips

- Do not wrap up things in a short period.
- The learning process should be based on a long-term course.
- Memory coding is a process of bottleneck phenomenon which usually takes 30-45 minutes for proper remembering.
- Try to learn things with less quantity at a time, and continue to learn over a long period.
- If you try to learn many things at a time it will add to your stress and your learning process would be deranged.

Discuss what you read last, with your friends. This will revise your subject and also if you are missing anything or wrongly remembering can be corrected by your friends.

Try to appear in all class terminal examinations, tuition examinations, and with similar pattern examination in your home. This will improve your understanding regarding question answers and build your confidence better for focusing on the examination.

- Just before (a few days before) the examination appears in mock examination in the particular subject which you want to improve. The pattern of examinations should be exactly the same as the real examination. This will reduce the examination phobia, stress, anxiety and your performance will be improved. The mock examination should be in a place where would be no disturbance. If you are mentally prepared for the mock examination and your study and revision are OK, then only you sit in this examination, otherwise, a failure here would be seriously distressing for the real examination.

- Any query, confusion, inquisition should directly be clarified in the class without any hesitation with the help of teachers, mentors. This will reduce your anxiety and with less effort, you can achieve more.

- There may be some difficult topics in all or some subjects. You should not ignore those and keep it for the examination time, as this will increase gradually and add on to your stress. So the difficult topics as and when required should be clarified without late.

- Sometimes many students get to benefit from **group discussions** for difficult subjects. Students should decide the time and subject for discussion. This will invariably help in remembering. If any student is not getting improvement he/she should take another way.

- After the completion of each revision period, make a short note of the topic and match it with others. See if you have missed anything, then you can take notes from others and correct those.

- Do not delay too long for revising difficult things.

- Note down points which you can remember easily of the difficult topics while revising.

- Underline important points in your notebook and highlight those if possible for immediate and improved recollection in mind.

- Note down the key points for better remembering (Brainstorming).

Make the Contents Brief

a. Form mnemonics, new words for difficult answers.

b. Make **links** to your topic. Briefly write down a ten-page topic in half a page.

c. For final examinations, you should refer to the text paper book which does contain all subjects. It is better to divide the bulky text paper book into different parts for each subject.

d. For each subject make a small note pad that can easily be carried in your pocket and note down important points, theories, formulae, laws. This would again help you in revising during examination time.

e. Put a small paper marker to demarcate that you have finished revising the topic or a portion.

Points listed from (a) to (e) will give you a sense of your progress and this is good for de-stressing yourself for examination.

- Do not revise the entire subject just before few days of examination. Only revise the topic you need.
- Make your own notes with relevant words and sentences which mean the most to you.
- Listen to audio and visual aids of the topic.
- Small notes in a pocket pad may be referred to as and when required.
- Talk to your senior students who have passed the examination regarding how to be successful in the examination.

Recognize examination stress and find a solution.

- Stress is the Psycho – Physiological reaction to an external unusual stimulus.
- It creates Fight & Flight reaction and also biochemical changes in the brain.
- Observe the slightest stress and from the beginning deal with it. Otherwise, a cumulative effect will make difficult situations.
- Take a balanced diet, adequate water, chocolates that have cardioprotective, antioxidant, and calming properties.

- Take mildly warm milk before sleep. It has got a sedating property.
- Adequate night sleep is essential.
- Interrupted sleep is normal. If it is more during the examination, do not worry otherwise the day following will become more stressful for you. So be relaxed always. Switch off lights before you sleep.
- Avoid taking alcohol and smoking as these add on to stress levels by increasing blood pressure and deranging brain chemical levels of adrenaline, noradrenaline, etc.

General issues to consider.

- Even if there is a negative thought, apprehension regarding the examination think positively that you qualified to join the course, so you can also qualify to pass this examination.
- Think that you have passed other examinations before.
- So you have that much intelligence to pass the coming examination.
- Do not hope for sudden success. Try for gradual improvement.
- Do daily relaxation like; a DMR, walking, meditation, night (hot/cold) bath, and listening to slow and classical music for a few minutes.
- The early morning bath is good for the day.
- Take a non-spicy breakfast.

Concerns for the examination

- Do a timely form fill up for the examination.
- Timely collect your examination card and necessary documents.
- Find out the exact place, building, room, and your seat for the examination if possible. This will reduce your last moment of stress and save time.
- Reach the examination hall a few minutes before the start of the examination.

- Enter the examination hall and sit in your place quietly for some time and then collect the question and answer papers. Write down in proper places your roll number, name, and subject name, and paper number.
- Take all those writing materials like pen, pencil, markers, eraser, scale, compass box, etc.
- Read the question paper in detail.
- Divide time for each answer.
- It is obvious that everyone gets a little nervous during the examination but do not worry about that. This will increase your body's performance by increasing a little adrenaline level.
- However, increased nervousness which your mental state cannot cope is definitely harmful.
- If you have distressing mental conditions talk to your examination supervisors and later after you finish the paper you may consult a doctor.
- Carefully read the instructions for answering which are mentioned in the question and answer sheets.
- Take a relaxing deep breath and look at the watch and start answering the question which looks easier to you to start with.
- If your time is spent more in one answer than your planned time, revise your time table again.
- If you find time is running out, for a few answers you can just mention the important points in your answer.
- **Know that no one is perfect and hence do not try to do everything perfectly. Just do what you know.**
- If you are more stressed about the examination, think that examination is not the end of everything. It is just a fraction of your carrier. Be relaxed and talk to yourself silently with a few relaxing words.

Incomplete Retrieval

If you find difficulty in retrieving an answer which you know, do not put your head forcibly on it to retrieve. Leave it. Go on to another question answer. In the meantime when you recollect the answer of the forgotten one come over to it.

- If it is possible, write key words of the answer in the first few lines. In the last few lines just make a summary of the answer only if time permits.
- Keep little space for writing a few lines in between two answers. In the end, if you have time you can write some additional relevant content.
- You can use some colour pens for underlining headings (only if colour pens are allowed).
- Make sure to number the pages of the answer papers and additional papers if you take them. Write your name and roll number in one corner of each page or at the given place.
- Tie the extra bunch of papers with the main answer sheet with a small thread or the supplied material.
- Try not to look here and there frequently. Only when you want to relax or retrieve something for few seconds look into the sky through the windows.
- After you get the question papers and answer sheets only be a concern with those.
- Think that for every success you need to do a little more.
- No failure is permanent.
- No failure is the end of life.
- Many people who have failed in their life also living happily at present.
- No point in worrying much either in anticipation of a failure or past failures.

- If you become very restless, talk to the examination supervising team and for sure they can help you to alleviate your stress.
- After failures, you can have a sweet success.

For a better result in the examination:

- Prepare for the examination adequately.
- Do not be stressed because of minor things.
- Do not postpone your studies.
- Do not be overconfident.
- Do not be in a negative mind.
- Plan for a small party or a holiday after the examination.

Anxiety (A Dynamic Approach)

Definition – The effect of fear is the unconscious detection of threats (Damasio-1999).

- The emotion of fear refers to the unconscious activation of the body by the somatic and autonomic nervous system (Damasio-1999).
- Anxiety is the fear triggered by our feelings.
- Anxiety is the feeling of threat. We can just rationalize it and reduce it by using our defence mechanisms.

Fear mobilizes the body to protect it physically (Parksepp-1998), whereas **anxiety mobilizes** us to defend ourselves psychologically (S. Freud).

What Anxiety Does:

- Gives signal to body of threats.
- Prepares the body to act accordingly.

Anxiety acts in the following ways:

1. Assessing danger instantly and sending a message to deal with it biologically to the amygdala.
2. The amygdala activates the SNS and ANS creating fear and emotions. The SNS activates the body muscles (voluntary) and as a result, we get a **fight and flight** response. The ANS balances with SNS by creating internal body vital organ functions appropriately.
3. To reduce the threat we use our defence mechanisms.

4. Consciously we adopt the symptoms of fear and threat as anxiety.

Dynamics of Anxiety: How It Presents and How to Resolve

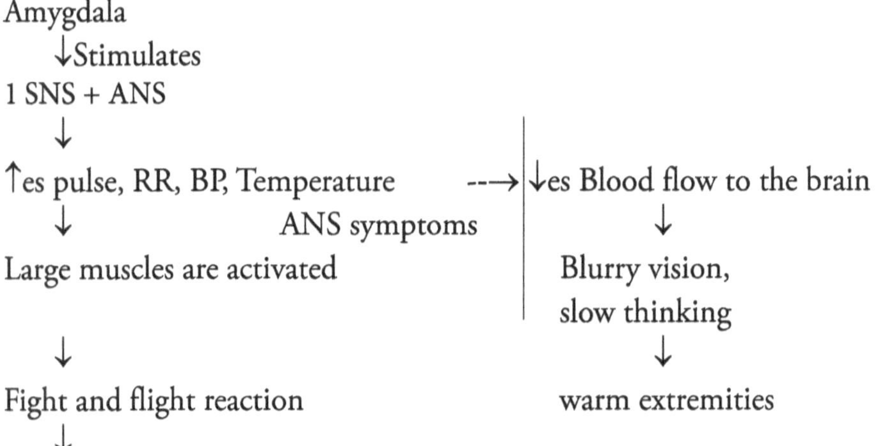

The SNS and ANS create the symptoms of anxiety before we consciously think about the threat even in less than a second.

- Fear can be adaptive to an objective threat. Fear can be a maladaptive reaction due to a misperception.
- Anxiety aggravates when the interpersonal relationship with others is low.

Unconscious cues → Amygdala and hypothalamus
                              ↓
          Corrective feedback ← Alarm
                 (Bodily symptoms)
2 Amygdala sends impulses → Prefrontal cortex
                   ↓
       Thinking and decision-making process
                   ↓
       Anxiety symptoms reduced

Past emotional threats act like unconscious threats and thus create more anxiety (Because those emotional issues are difficult to retrieve).

Example of → **Anxiety**

A recent examination is a cure for anxiety.

3 Death of a first-order relative before the examination.

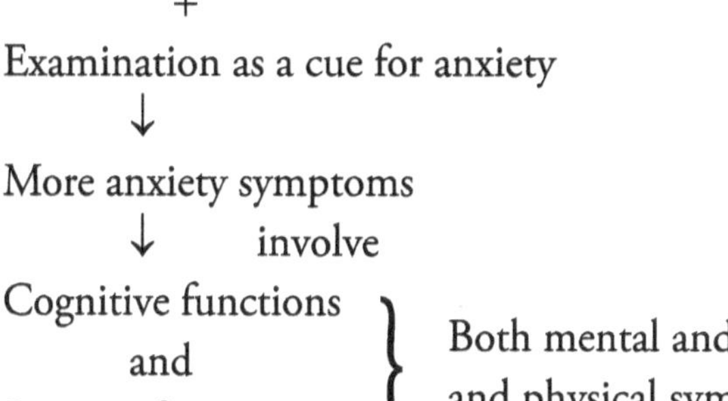

4. Anxiety symptoms occur before higher cognitive functions appear.

Anxiety provoking situations are countered by **pre-prepared behaviour**. Example –

Sudden closure of eyelids in anticipation of an external object falling into the eye.

Sudden closure of eyelids is a prepared behaviour.

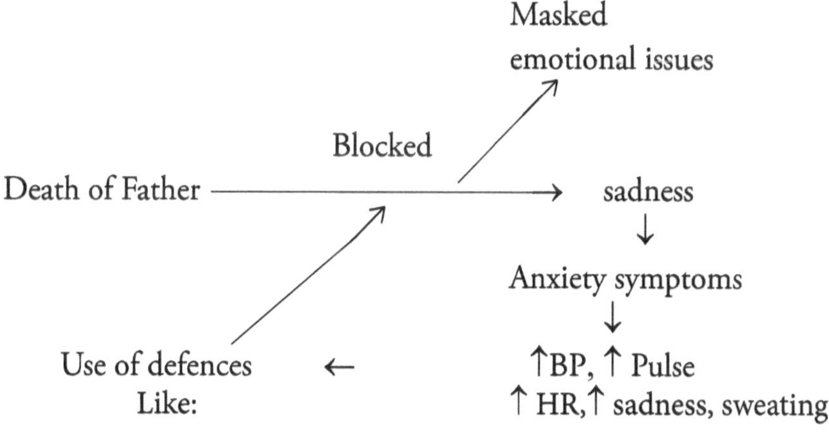

5.   1. Displacement
         2. Rationalization
         3. Comparison
         4. Systemic de-stressing.

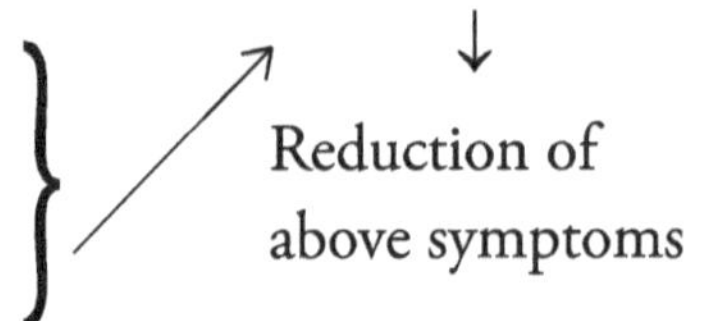

Reduction of
above symptoms

Anxiety is Not a Stimulus

Few theories having contradicting meaning:

1.   Separation anxiety → loss of loved one
2.   Castration anxiety → damage to genitals
3.   Moral anxiety → transgressing personal values
4.   Annihilation anxiety → being destroyed
5.   Persecutory anxiety → feelings of being hurt by others

The above are only stimuli, not anxiety (Waelder 1960).

Anxiety is Not a Thought

Abusing with threatening words create anger and then anxious reaction starts in the body; then the realization of the whole process starts. This subsequently creates the use of defence mechanisms and these are thoughts only.

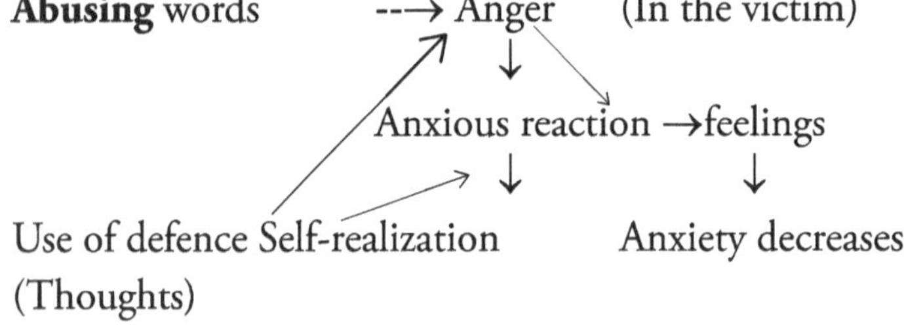

Anxiety is an unconscious biological reaction of the body because of an external stimulus.

Symptoms of Anxiety

Somatic – clenched hands, headache, body pain, stomach ache, menstrual irregularity, lose motion, increased urination.

Sympathetic – Dry mouth, dry eyes, dilated pupil, cold hands, increased HR, BP, RR, blushing, GI motility increased, shivering, etc.

Parasympathetic – salivation, teary eyes, constricted pupil, warm hands, decreased-HR, BP, RR and diarrhoea, dizziness, confusion.

Unconscious Anxiety Discharge

If anxiety is regulated properly, it is released from cognitive functions to the striated muscles.

Anxiety   --→   Regulated   --→   improved   Cognitive functions   --→   thinking improves
  --→   striated muscles relaxed
↓
BP, HR, RR, warmth of the body
are normalized.

* **Therapist role**: If the patient can observe his anxiety tell him to find out the feelings behind anxiety or help him to follow the process of anxiety stepwise and find out the feelings.

Tell the patient to identify the defences that prevent anxiety. If the patient cannot observe his anxiety and regulate it then he is likely to use defence mechanisms frequently.

Stages of Anxiety Dynamics

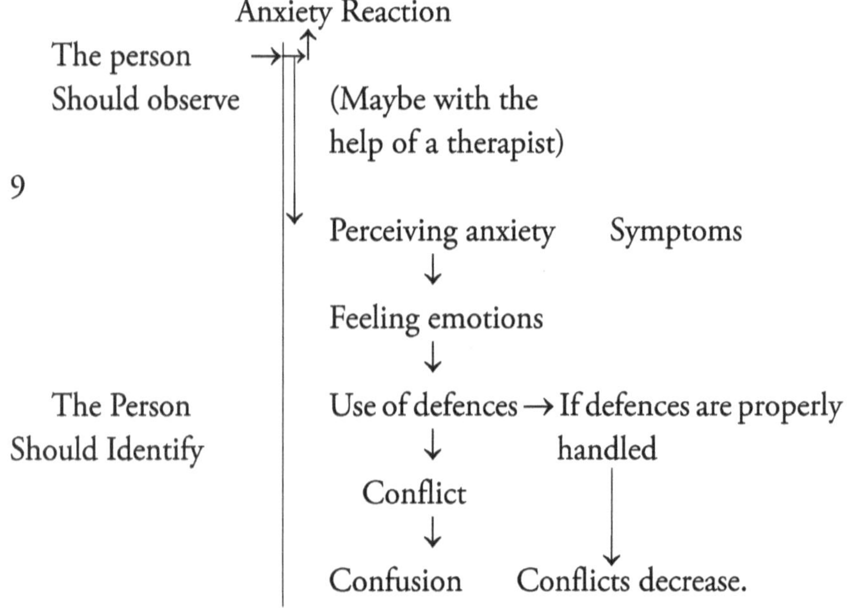

Unconscious Feelings of Anxiety

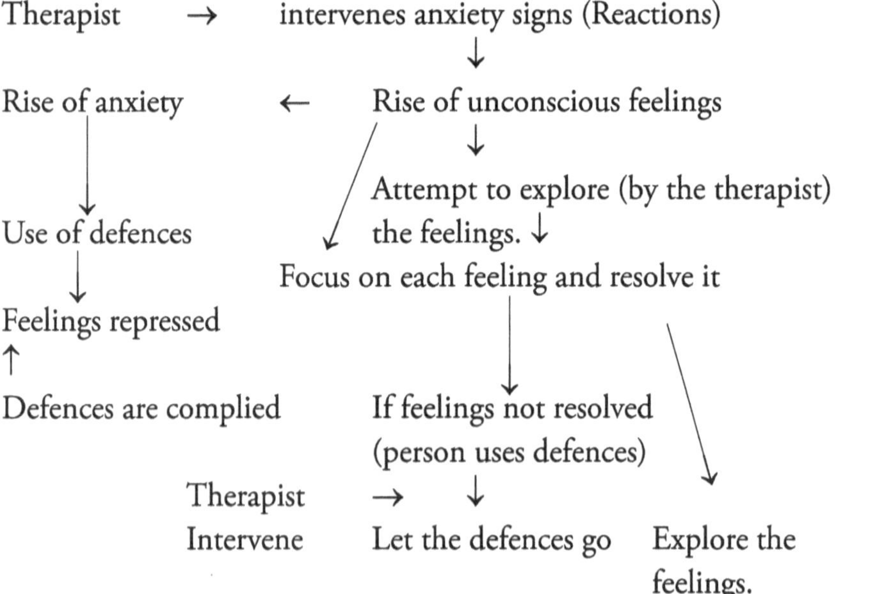

Ways of Anxiety Discharge

1. High anxiety tolerance (striated muscle affected)
    ↓
    Present fewer anxiety symptoms
    ↓
    Sigh, tense (striated muscle signs)
    Licking lips, dry mouth

2. Low anxiety tolerance:
    (smooth muscle affected)
    High anxiety → dry mouth, ↑ HR, ↑PR, ↑ RR, nausea, headache, migraine
    ↓
    Defences used are regressive defences like projection

3. Much prior to the counselling session too much of the threshold for anxiety tolerance is already exceeded.

    - Patients feel smooth muscle functioning impairment.
    - Cognitive impairment.
    - Perceptual impairment

4. Highly exceeding the threshold for anxiety tolerance

    - Low tension in the body → less or nil restless feelings, no clenching of hands.
    - Flat affect, flat tone, thoracic breathing.
    - Cognitive functions are significantly impaired – high levels of endorphins are responsible for this. Here the anxiety discharge into smooth muscles.
    - Now if the client is not intervened and made aware that he is having anxiety in some form, then he will use **regressive defence mechanisms.**
    - Most severely anxious patients somehow think their problems will be increased by the therapist, because of poor rapport and projection (regressive defence).

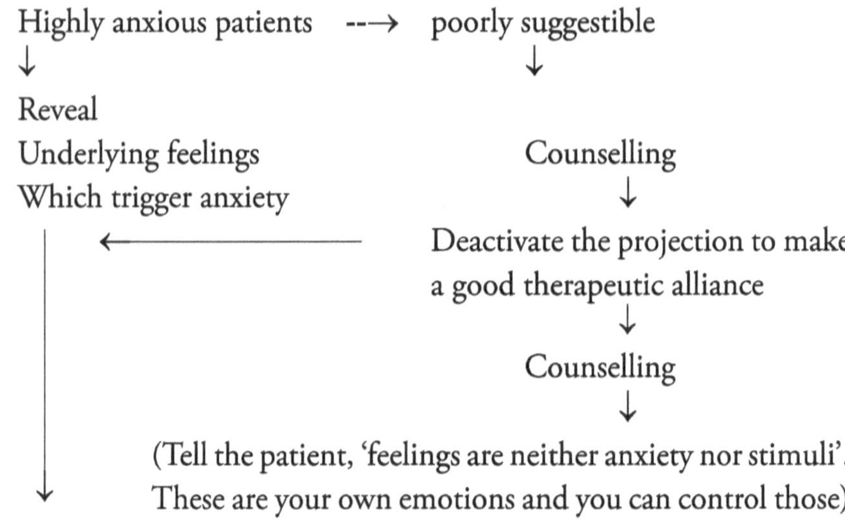

Once the patient realizes he is using projection or using some other regressive defence mechanisms and differentiates the therapist from it, then he will just freeze the earlier responses.

Freezing reaction blocks the past reactions.

Defences used by patients:

Angry   → Projection, Identification

Forgetful   → Repression

Freezing   → Reaction formation, differentiation

Procrastinating → Rationalization

Conflict   → Intellectualization

High anxiety precipitates cognitive and perceptual distortions:
Reasons:

1. Decreased blood flow to the brain.

2. Increase the release of neuro-hormones.

    (1) – Parasympathetic nervous system symptoms cause a sudden drop in blood flow in the brain stem, frontal lobe, Brocas area. This causes fainting attacks, postural hypotension, and altered consciousness.

                ↓   Amygdala function impaired.

Inability to inhibit Amygdala further (Because of cognitive
distortions)
↓
Fear response decreases

(2) – Increase release of neurohormones
↓
Increase levels of endorphins
↓
Decrease memory formation and coding, confusion, cognitive and perceptual distortions.

(3) – Increase cortisol
↓
Inhibit the function of the hippocampus
↓

Impairs – learning   } Confusion, cognitive and
    – self functioning } perceptual distortions.

(4) – Blood glucose from the hippocampus and other brain areas are diverted to the peripheral body (striated muscles).
↓

This creates anxious patients become lethargic – Inhibit memory retrieving and long-term memory formation cognitive distortions.

(5) – Experiencing anxiety feelings to the maximum till it is discharged into striated muscles, is the anxiety Threshold.

    Anxiety   → released to striated muscles
↓

smooth muscles ← still too much of
anxiety persisting
↓

Now the patient perceives cognitive and perceptual disturbances.
↓

This means the anxiety has gone beyond the Threshold level.

↓

Needs Therapy

* Therapy/counselling can be given at any stage of anxiety when the client is suggestible for counselling and presents with good judgement.

Resolving Anxiety

Always notice your anxiety, the feelings.

Find out the stimulus.

Differentiate your feelings of anxiety from the defence mechanism you use to control those.

Break defences first and after that, you can control anxiety

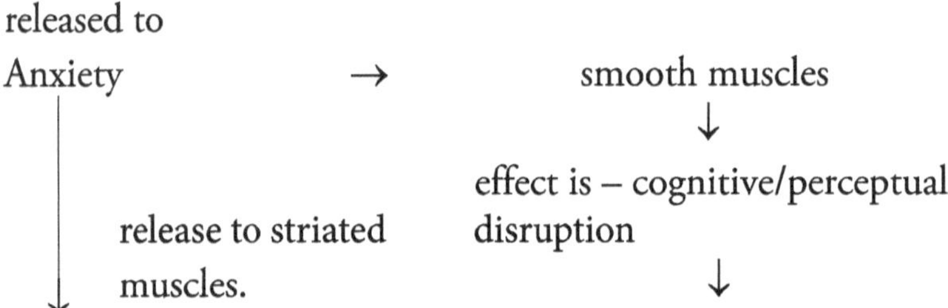

released to

Anxiety   →   smooth muscles
                                                        ↓
                                           effect is – cognitive/perceptual
             release to striated   disruption
             muscles.   ↓

Let the anxiety go to the striated muscles and now stop exploring feelings.

Repeat the cycle till the Anxiety is reduced
↓
Explore the feelings

By repeating the above cycle the patient builds tolerance for the feelings and reduces the Regressive Defences.

When anxiety moves into smooth muscles the cognitive and perceptual functions become distorted. Now the therapist guides the client the following:

- Not to explore the feelings now. Because the cognitive functions are impaired, so the power of Judgement would be poor.
- Make aware of the client his anxiety symptoms.

- Let the anxiety symptoms release to striated muscles so that the client now can go into the feelings
- Allow him to see sequentially stimulus, feelings, anxiety (reactions), and symptoms.
- Rehearse the symptoms.
- Then explore the feelings.

Tell the patient that

- Feelings trigger anxiety.
- To create self-observing capacity in the patient during anxiety.
- Ignoring anxiety will remain unregulated.
- To let go of defences. Because these defences distract the patient from paying attention to his anxiety. If the patient can let the defences go, the patient can judge the feelings and anxiety can be regulated.
- Not to use defences to pacify anxiety.
- To feel the bodily feelings.
- Anxiety and its bodily symptoms hold meaning in the past, present, and future but only can be controlled in the present, not in the past or future.
- Use of Defence Mechanisms impairs anxiety management.
- Always a precondition is required to create a change in the relationship.
- Even if the therapist tells the patient that you are moving your feet continuously while sitting and this is a symptom of anxiety and if the patient wants to ignore it he will tell I do like this all the time (Rationalization, intellectualization). Tell the patient that you are using defences which you should not, for a conscious act of resolving anxiety. Tell the patient that ignoring anxiety is not good for therapy if the patient is under the process of therapy). So then the patient might realize his feelings of anxiety and then the therapeutic alliance would be good. Finally, the therapy will move forward.

- Allow the patient to realize that he is using defences to ignore the anxiety and create a feeling 'this is not good'.
- Tell the patient to observe the current happenings.
- Tell the patient if you ignore "now", your anxiety will be multiplied. Block the defences "now", preventing it to go to the future.
- Ask the patient this question – If you ignore your anxiety "now" how it will help you in the future?
- Tell the patient to remain in the present and feel the anxiety. Future hopes and remembering past traumas will always trigger anxiety.

  - Spot on to the present moment.
  - Feelings (of anxiety) always create unconscious reactions.
  - Notice the type of bodily reaction that is occurring because of unconscious threat.
  - Know that defences reduce anxiety but the severity increases in the future. So do not use defences and if used earlier, break those by counselling. (with the help of a therapist).
  - Anxiety is triggered by – objective dangers (A. Freud – 1936), and unconscious cues (S. Freud – 1926).

Steps of the circle of anxiety and defence mechanism:

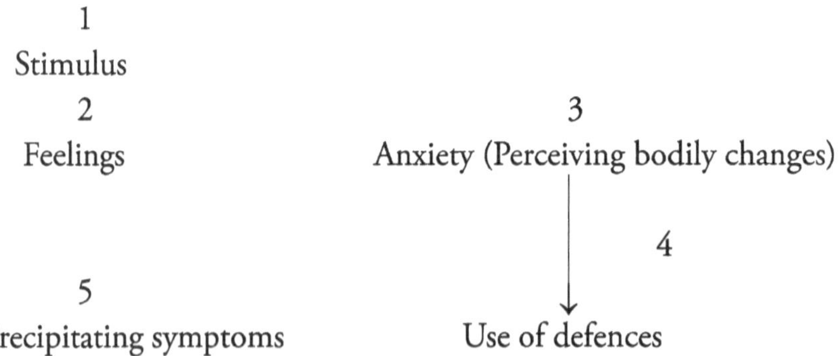

Some defences do not repress but perpetuate anxiety, like – Identification.

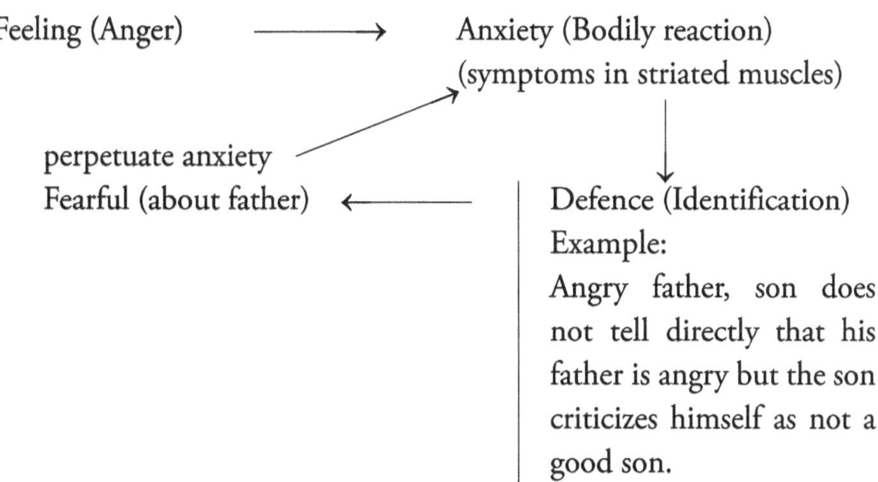

(Son enacts Identification and identification is the superego function.

The above example is superego anxiety.

Superego anxiety is self-attack and this seriously increases anxiety (A. Freud – 1936).

Distraction in the self-observing capacity of feelings increases anxiety.

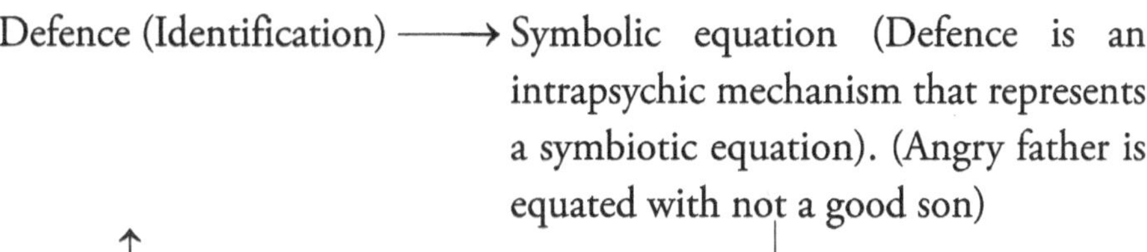

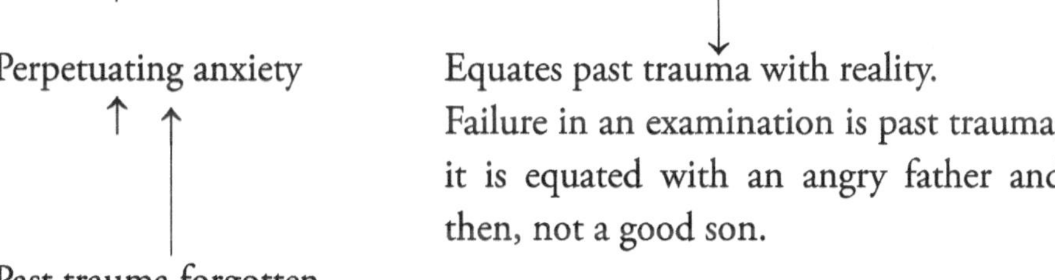

'Not a good son' Segal – 1981. Failure in an examination is past trauma, is pushed into the subconscious, and 'not a good son' (current reality).

In a symbolic equation, rationalization, and projection, to resolve all these defences few other factors should be looked after, like:

Time – Past, present, and future.

Place.

Differentiate the reality from the meaning of defences.

One of the major reasons why anxiety persists is the inability to differentiate fantasy, imageries from reality.

The reality in a distorted functioning always increases imageries and fantasies and that leads to precipitate more severe anxiety.

Reference Books

1. Comprehensive Text Book of Psychiatry – VI – Kaplan, Sadock
2. Introduction to Psychology – Seventh Edition
   – Morgan, King, Weisz, Schopler
3. The ICD – 10 – Classification of Mental and Behavioural Disorders
   – WHO
4. Co-Creating Change
   – Jon Fredericson